— A —
Lutheran Toolkit

— A —
Lutheran
Toolkit

Ken
Sundet
Jones

A Lutheran Toolkit

All Scripture quotations, unless otherwise indicated, are taken from New Revised Standard Version Bible, copyright © 1989 National Council of the Churches of Christ in the United States of America. Used by permission. All rights reserved worldwide.

Scripture quotations marked (NIV) are taken from the Holy Bible, New International Version®, NIV®. Copyright © 1973, 1978, 1984, 2011 by Biblica, Inc.™ Used by permission of Zondervan. All rights reserved worldwide. www.zondervan.com The "NIV" and "New International Version" are trademarks registered in the United States Patent and Trademark Office by Biblica, Inc.™

Published by:
1517 Publishing
PO Box 54032
Irvine, CA 92619-4032

Publisher's Cataloging-In-Publication Data
(Prepared by The Donohue Group, Inc.)

Names: Jones, Ken Sundet, author.
Title: A Lutheran toolkit / Ken Sundet Jones.
Description: Irvine, CA : 1517 Publishing, [2021] | Includes bibliographical references.
Identifiers: ISBN 9781948969444 (paperback) | ISBN 9781948969451 (ebook)
Subjects: LCSH: Lutheran Church—Doctrines. | Lutheran Church—History. | God (Christianity) | Christian life.
Classification: LCC BX8065.3 .J66 2021 (print) | LCC BX8065.3 (ebook) | DDC 230.41—dc23

Printed in the United States of America

Cover art by Brenton Clarke Little
Author photo by Todd Bailey

For Ryan and all my students who've had ears to hear and hearts for the gospel, and with thanks to Jim and Gerhard, who handed on what they'd been given

Contents

Introduction...ix

1. Looking for God in the Void.................. 1

2. Sin (Uppercase and Lowercase) and the
   Captive Will 11

3. Starting with Christ, the God Who
   Shows Up.................................. 23

4. Justification by Faith........................ 29

5. Delivering the Goods........................ 37

6. Being Made New............................ 45

7. The Church? I Don't Even Know What
   the Church Is Anymore..................... 53

8. The Word Made Visible...................... 61

9. Sacraments Valid and Effective............... 69

10. It'll Be the Death of You 79

Introduction

A Lutheran toolkit? First, what it is: it's shorthand for a set of questions and outlooks that guide us in our thinking about what God does for us in the person of Jesus Christ. Second, what it's not: it's not an advertisement for any Lutheran church body over or against some other denomination. In keeping with the Reformer, Martin Luther himself, being Lutheran isn't about institutions or organizations. Instead, it's a way of looking at life, reading scripture, hearing God, and living a Christian life.

Tools are objects that serve to obtain a desired outcome. Hammers help build the places we live in, wrenches help put together the bicycle your kid got for Christmas, and mops help us clean up kitchen messes. In the same way, the Lutheran toolkit contains things with a particular end in mind—to create and sustain saving faith. In short, the toolkit is about how and why the gospel gets proclaimed, along with how it changes what we think it means to be a faithful person in this world.

The first tools we'll grab out of the box are really two parts of one tool, like the two parts of a pair of pliers or scissors. They tell us why we even need a toolkit and what kind of box all these Lutheran tools nestle in (in case you're wondering, it's Christ himself). We'll talk about the hidden and revealed God. Then we'll pick up the idea of sin as a way of talking about how we human beings confront our outrage that God wants to be in charge, and along the way we'll chuck out the tool of free will as a fairly useless implement that doesn't live up to its late-night infomercials. Two well-known Lutheran tools, justification by faith and law-and-gospel thinking, will show how God actually works to free us from sin and build up new lives in us. The sacraments of baptism and the Lord's Supper will show the concrete means that God uses for the task of fighting the problem of our lack of faith. Finally, we'll take up a little-known and under-appreciated tool that's usually lost in the pile of screwdrivers at the back of the box. However, this tool, vocation, is one of the best ways to describe how Christians live for God and their neighbors, and it's one that looks different from what most people might expect to find in our toolkit.

Along the way, you'll gain some historical background about where this stuff came from in Luther's life and work and the history of the Reformation. We'll dig into some key passages in the Bible that Luther relied on and that highlight what the various tools can be used for.

When we close the lid on the box, you will be able to grab the handle and take it with you. Then the Lutheran toolkit will keep you focused on a clear picture of who Christ is for you, how God can use you to create that same relationship with others (especially those closest to you), and how you are freed to live within that relationship in your everyday life. And it might become something you can lay your hands on when you're called to account for your faith or asked to explain why you don't seem to fit in with those who've drunk the world's Kool-Aid.

Acknowledgments extend to three places: First, many thanks to the staff and campers at Outlaw Ranch, a Lutheran Bible camp in the Black Hills of South Dakota, and to a number of Iowa congregations. This project began as a series of presentations given to a group of faithful adults during a week of family camp, which itself has a place of primacy in my own faith history. Later, the lectures were modified and presented to adult education groups at Luther Memorial Church, St. John's Lutheran Church, St. Mark Lutheran Church, and Faith Lutheran Church in the Des Moines metro area, as well as First Lutheran Church in Cedar Rapids. In each case, the participants provided helpful feedback and, more importantly, showed ears finely tuned to the gospel.

A second set of thanks goes to Grand View University, its board of trustees, president, and provost. The initial tool-kit presentations began to be molded into book form during a sabbatical semester in which I was released from teaching, committee service, and duties in the Theology and Philosophy Department. The sabbatical offered me time and space to take up my scholarly vocation. These ideas have percolated over the span of more than a decade and, semester after semester, have appeared in one form or another in course lectures and conversations with the hundreds of students who have sat through a term in my classroom. The chance to pull it all together in this project is a gift indeed.

Many thanks for my brothers and sisters in Christ at 1517. I began my connection with 1517 by being delighted with the faithful and theologically reliable work I encountered online. Now that I've added to it through regular opportunities to be an evangelist and teacher on the website, to speak at Christ Hold Fast, and to attend the annual Here We Still Stand conference, my delight and gratitude have grown through the relationships with 1517 staff. In particular, I've cherished time spent with Scott and Joy Keith, Kelsi Klembara, Daniel Emery Price, Chad Bird, and so many others.

Finally, I thank the faithful five who listen and speak to me daily. My trusted colleagues Mark Mattes and Kathryn Duffy and my campus pastor Russell Lackey—all fine friends and grace-hardened sinners—have shaped this material in untold ways. And the greatest thanks go to my wife and son, Mary and Sam, whose patient interest gird me, whose clever wit and clear eyes enlarge me, and whose abiding care sustains me. All of them have allowed me to open this toolkit time and again, calibrating and honing the tools within to unlock grace and faith.

Chapter 1

Looking for God in the Void

Everyone has played hide-and-seek as a kid, but there is a variation that is even more fun. It is called Sardines. Instead of everyone hiding and one person having to find them all, in Sardines, only one person hides and everyone goes looking. When you find the person hiding, you hide with them. Eventually the hiding place fills up with the finders, and too many people are crammed into a too-small space. Hence the game's name: Sardines. And its good fun until the hider finds some impossible nook and can't be found. Then the game devolves into a bunch of grumpy people wandering around frustrated. Sardines is only fun if the hider can be found.

    When I was in junior high, I had only really been connected to the church for a few years. I knew that when I died, God would take a look at my record and decide whether to send me to heaven or hell. I sure tried to be good, and I thought I was a nice kid—at least compared to my school bullies. But I was clueless about what God actually thought of me. I remember lying in my twin bed after turning out the lights, terrified to fall asleep lest I hadn't asked forgiveness for all my sins. If I didn't and died before I woke, I'd be consigned to hell for eternity. That's the problem we human creatures have with God. We look for God's presence in our lives and want to know whether we stand in God's favor. But the game only leads to a kind of existential terror because we seek a God who hides.

Looking for God is a good and noble quest, but God sometimes loves camouflage and out-of-the-way places. God is usually hiding far out of sight, impossible to track down. And when the burdens of life come bearing down and you most need to hear from God, you find even your most heartfelt prayers echo back with silence. If God is going to mean anything to you, you must find a way to talk about who God is and what God does. How is it possible for you to say anything about God?

When the evangelical Reformers were called to Augsburg in 1530 to defend their teachings before the emperor and representatives of the church, they presented a document drafted by Martin Luther's colleague, Philip Melanchthon, at the University of Wittenberg. That document has come to be known as the Augsburg Confession. It's one of the main sources Lutherans look to when they say what they believe. Melanchthon began his statement with an article called "Concerning God." He said he and his fellow Reformers taught that God was the Trinity: Father, Son, and Holy Spirit. And he said that God is "eternal, undivided, unending, of immeasurable power, wisdom, and goodness, the creator and preserver of all visible and invisible things."[1] Melanchthon's words assume that you *can* say something about God (we call it "theology"), and what you come up with is the foundation for everything else. The question of how you know these

---

[1]   Philip Melanchthon, "The Augsburg Confession," in *The Book of Concord: The Confessions of the Evangelical Lutheran Church*, ed. Robert Kolb and Timothy J. Wengert (Minneapolis: Fortress, 2000), 36.

things helps us understand more about who God is, why Christ comes to us, and what the church is for.

Five years earlier, in 1525, Luther was in a fierce battle of ideas with the great humanist thinker Erasmus of Rotterdam. In *The Bondage of the Will*, his response to Erasmus's attack, Luther said that Erasmus was the only sparring partner who had ever landed on the most important questions at issue in the Reformation. Erasmus had begun his side of the argument in his *Diatribe on Free Will* by saying that Luther was wrong to make so many assertions about God. He said the scriptures are just too murky to make full sense of them, and having someone at the head of the church in Rome helped. God had designated the pope and given him the gifts to do the explaining and asserting for us.

Human beings have long tried to make sensible assertions about the world around us and about God as well. The ancient philosophers who were working before Socrates came on the scene in Greece (people with difficult names like Anaxagoras and Anaximenes, and don't get me started on Xenophanes and Anaximander) sought something they could say with absolute certainty. They looked at the world around them and saw that everything was constantly changing. They wanted to put their finger on something that didn't change, no matter what. One thinker said it was air, another that it was water, still another that it was fire. Pythagoras—he of the famous theorem—said the one unchangeable thing was that everything was made of numbers. When we assert anything about the natural world, the only information we have to go on comes from our five senses. You could look at a campfire and see how the logs become ashes and release heat and light, and then you might say that's how the whole world changes. If that's so, then fire must be the most elemental thing in the world.

But although God is in the world, God is not of the world. You can't use your senses to access God. There's a wide

gap between God and you. Like Erasmus, even though you
have scripture to guide you and give you some information,
the weather in this world of thought is still partly cloudy. If
you tried to assert something absolutely true about God, it
would be a frustrating task, especially if you tried to do
it without saying anything about Jesus or without asserting
anything you were not sure of. Even the most basic assertion
in First John that "God is love" (4:8) isn't something you can
have any certainty about or can put forth apart from how
God has come to us in Christ. (Be patient. We will get to him
in a bit.) To say anything about God's mercy or forgiveness
is just as hard. And the most basic question about whether
God exists is the most difficult of all. Although atheist writers
have made plenty of hay arguing that you can't ever come up
with satisfying, irrefutable proof of God's existence, plenty
of Christian thinkers through the ages have tried.

One classic proof of God has its roots in the Golden
Age of ancient Greece. The philosopher Aristotle tried to
understand what causes things to happen. He said that every
movement has a cause. I ate some red beans and rice for supper last night, which was caused by my hunger, which was
caused by my using up carbs and proteins as I moved around
all day, which was caused by my needing to work, which was
caused by having to pay school loans, which was caused by
28 years of education, which was caused by something else,
which was caused by something else. Eventually we will get
to a point where we land on a first cause—something that
started it all moving without being caused by something else,
an Unmoved Mover. In the Middle Ages, when Scholastic
theologians rediscovered Aristotle's philosophy, they read
his thoughts on causation, and when they encountered
the idea of the Unmoved Mover, they thought, "Hmmm.
Methinks he doth speak of God."

Another proof was Anselm's idea of God as the greatest
conceivable being. It goes like this: Your mind can conceive

of a being that is greater than anything else you can think of. This being has to be something real and not just something you've thought up. If such a being existed solely in your mind, then it would be possible to think of it as existing in reality as well. A real being would then be greater than the one that merely exists in your mind. That would contradict your first idea and be impossible, which means that the first being actually exists both in your mind and in reality. And that being is God.

These thinkers used their rational minds, rather than their five senses, to find a way to say something about God's existence that meets our criteria—we can't refer to Jesus or say something we're not absolutely sure of. But the problem with these proofs is that once you get yourself a provable God, it leaves way bigger questions standing there: If this God exists, how do you know who that God is? Is this God actually good? In the end, what will God's judgment on you be? All the questions and proofs force a difficult realization on you: using your senses and your rational mind, you can't truly know anything about God's existence, actions, or attitudes toward you. And you wind up with my Twin Bed Theological Terrors.

If you try to suss it out by looking at the world around you, you might say you have found evidence in nature. The breathtaking beauty of a sunset, a rainbow, the variety of snowflakes and human faces, and the way harmony works in music—all these things show us both God's existence and his goodness. You can add plenty more to the list from your own experience, from the taste of ripe strawberries, to rumbling thunder, to the twinkling of a field of stars on a summer's night or that of your beloved's eyes. Yet it is not hard to find other scientific explanations for all these things that say nothing at all about God. What's more, if you want to use beautiful and amazing things as proof of God's existence or goodness, you also have to take with them all the bad things you see and experience in nature: natural disasters, cancer, the perils of toilet training, adolescent angst, and all those things insurance companies call "acts of God." Even if you could argue for God's existence, when you add these things to the mix, it becomes hard to say whether God is even good. Luther said this was the greatest temptation. Like him, you can get to the point where you say you "don't know if God is the devil or the devil is God."[2] And in our game of divine Sardines, God remains tucked away in some inaccessible eternal nook.

That is the exact confusion that crops up in the story of Adam and Eve in the Garden of Eden in Genesis 3. The temptation the serpent sets before the woman is *not* whether she and the man should eat the fruit of the tree of the knowledge of good and evil. Instead, the serpent asks whether they can trust God's motives in commanding them to keep away from the tree and God's judgment of death. The serpent says, "You will not die; for God knows that when you eat of it your eyes will be opened, and you will be like God, knowing good and evil" (Genesis 3:4b–5). Instead of trusting God to give them all that they needed for their creaturely existence, they turned to the serpent for its wisdom and to themselves as agents for concocting their future. They came to think that God was holding back something especially good. At best, they regarded God as their lackey and, at worst, their enemy. Thus our first parents and every generation after them have taken matters into their own hands.

That's what happens when God remains hidden behind the veil, when you can't grasp what God is up to, and when the threats and temptations of this world move you to seek certainty. You scramble to cobble together something sure

---

[2] Martin Luther, *D. Martin Luthers Werke: Kritische Ausgabe: Tischreden*, 6 vols., Weimarer ed. (Weimar: H. Böhlaus Nachfolger, 1912–21), 5:600, 11f, my translation.

that will give you security and hope. Luther knew something of such things when he wrote his explanation of the first article of the Apostles' Creed in the Small Catechism in 1529:

> I believe that God has created me together with all that exists. God has given me and still preserves my body and soul: eyes, ears, and all limbs and senses; reason and all mental faculties. In addition, God daily and abundantly provides shoes and clothing, food and drink, house and farm, spouse and children, fields, livestock, and all property—along with all the necessities and nourishment for this body and life. God protects me against all danger and shields and preserves me from all evil. And all this is done out of pure, fatherly, and divine goodness and mercy, without any merit or worthiness of mine at all![3]

This is nothing like the vast, terrifying power of a God who remains hidden. Luther came to know a God who is gracious, patient, and lavish in bestowing gifts. In fact, he argued that you could come to see God in creation, even in the hard facts of life and the terror of nature's perils. You could come to regard all these things as simple masks covering the face of God.

In the Old Testament, seeing God without a mask is a dangerous thing. When Moses and God's people were enslaved in Egypt and Pharaoh finally released them from bondage, they stood trapped at the sea with the Egyptian armies, with all their horses and charioteers, coming up behind them. God appeared behind the masks of a pillar of cloud by day and a pillar of fire by night. But when God gave the enemy armies a glimpse of divine might and glory, they were thrown into a panic. Their chariots were stuck, and

---

[3] Martin Luther, "The Small Catechism," in *Book of Concord*, 354–55.

people fled hither and yon—all from a wee glimpse behind the veil.

Later, when Moses was given the commandments on Mount Sinai, the mountain was clouded over, and the people below were protected from God's nearness. When Moses said to God, "Show me your glory," God said to Moses, "You cannot see my face; for no one shall see me and live" (Exodus 33:18–20). Moses was instructed to hide in a crack in the face of the rock, and Moses had to wait until God said "when." The most Moses was allowed to see was God's back, but still, when he came down from the mountain, Moses had been physically changed: "The skin of his face shone because he had been talking with God" (Exodus 34:29). Looking at the guy who had looked at God so spooked the Israelites that from that time forward, Moses took the clouded Mount Sinai as his model: he wore a veil over his head and only took it off when he went back to the summit to chat with the Lord.

The commandment-inscribed tablets that God gave Moses were placed in a golden ark, which was carried with the Israelites in their wilderness wanderings and in their conquest of the land God had promised them. The ark that contained these tablets that God's own hand had touched was so holy and so dangerous that when the Israelites moved their encampment, only the priests could come close, and the rest of the people were instructed to stay 1,000 yards away from it (Joshua 3:4). Years later, when the ark was being moved on an oxcart, the holy crate began to slip. A man named Uzzah reached out to steady it, and—Zap! Learn your lesson, Uzzah!—he was struck dead on the spot. King David heard of these things and was afraid to have the ark anywhere near him (1 Chronicles 13:9–14). When the temple was finally built in Jerusalem, the ark was installed in a space with floor-to-ceiling curtains surrounding it. The space was called the Holy of Holies, another way of saying it was the holiest of spaces. Ever. No one was allowed to enter except the high priest, and he could only do it on the Day of Atonement.

In the 1981 Steven Spielberg blockbuster, *Raiders of the Lost Ark*, the Nazi villains and the hero, Indiana Jones, are on a race to capture the Ark of the Covenant. The Nazis hope to harness its powers and use God as a weapon for Hitler and the Third Reich. At the climax of the movie, Indy and his companion Marion are themselves captured and bound while the Nazis intone the ancient words of the Israelite priests. As the villains lift the lid of the ark, Indy says, "Shut your eyes, Marion. Don't look at it, no matter what happens." The villains come to their end when the power and glory of God rise out of the ark and cause wholesale destruction: lightning-fried soldiers, melting faces, and exploding Nazi heads. But the protagonists are saved because they didn't look or come near.[4]

Of course, *Raiders* is a fiction, but in at least one way, it tells the truth: be careful about wanting to see an *un*hidden God. Even encountering God secondhand is dangerous stuff, and God will brook no attempts to get behind the veil. You won't get to crawl into God's hiding space and have other seekers cram in with you. The game of divine Sardines can't end. You're left to wander, grumpy and frustrated, and wonder what kind of God this is. You'll say, "Hidden God? No thanks. I'll stick with something I can see and trust."

And that's where Article I of the Augsburg Confession is in your corner. By including the language of the Holy Trinity (the Father, the Son, and the Holy Spirit), Philip Melanchthon points to the places God wants to be encountered and where faith can actually see God. And it gets even more specific. The article speaks of who Jesus is: both

---

[4] *Raiders of the Lost Ark*, directed by Steven Spielberg (1981; Los Angeles: Paramount Pictures, 2003), DVD.

completely divine and wholly human. That means that in this person, Jesus of Nazareth, you have access to a God who is overflowing with loving kindness for broken and sinful human creatures. It means that God has determined to call everyone in from hiding, "Olly olly oxen free." Or as Paul said in Galatians, "For freedom Christ has set us free" (5:1).

Chapter 2

Sin (Uppercase and Lowercase) and the Captive Will

We have already begun to see the results of playing Sardines with God. No matter how hard we seek, God stays hidden, and we human beings are not very good at being unsuccessful game players. In the Augsburg Confession, right after Philip Melanchthon tells us about God's existence in Article I, he immediately moves to the consequences of our frustrated quest to get behind God's veil. He tells us all about Sin:

> It is taught among us that since the fall of Adam, all human beings who are born in the natural way are conceived and born in sin. This means that from birth they are full of evil lust and inclination and cannot by nature possess true fear of God and true faith in God. Moreover, this same innate disease and original sin is truly sin and condemns to God's eternal wrath all who are not in turn born anew through baptism and the Holy Spirit.[1]

---

[1] Melanchthon, "Augsburg Confession," 36, 38.

That is a mouthful, and it sounds a lot like the fire-and-brimstone preaching of the New England Puritan preacher Jonathan Edwards in his famous sermon "Sinners in the Hands of an Angry God." It's not something that sits well on our ears. Whether it is the mother who inspired a tattoo or a preacher hovering above you in a pulpit, we don't like a wagging finger, scolding words, or scowling eyes looking across a pair of spectacles.

In the years before I went to seminary, I served as a youth minister in Dawson, a little town on Highway 212 in western Minnesota. During my last summer in that congregation, the American Lutheran Church had a national youth gathering in Denver. We had a goodly batch of kids ready to go, but there were two ninth-grade boys I had my doubts about. I knew that when it came down to it, Ricky and Jay would always forsake the group and go their own way. Not such a bad thing in a town of 2,000 surrounded by soybean fields. But I wasn't sure that would be wise for two guys who imagined they were bigger than the Mile-High City. I found a program that Lutherhaven, one of our Bible camps in Idaho, was offering. It was a design-your-own high adventure experience, and we opted for a small-scale white-water rafting trip. While the rest of the kids were busing out to Colorado, we hopped in my standard transmission Plymouth Reliant and trekked to Salmon, Idaho, to meet our camp staff member and our two rafting guides for six days on the Salmon River—more affectionately known as the River of No Return.

It was just the six of us heading down that amazing canyon, alternating between churning rapids and eerily languid stretches. At the end of the first day, we pulled our raft onto a sandbar at the river's edge and set up camp. Our guide Bucky told Ricky and Jay they could splash around in the water but that they could not go farther than knee-deep. He said that even though it looked calm, the river was dangerously deceptive. The current was so strong that it would grab you and sweep you around the bend to the next rapids, and there was nothing you could do about it. I trusted that Ricky and Jay would be obedient, but as I was setting up my tent, I heard shouts from the river. My two boys had decided to swim across to a sand beach on the opposite bank, and the current had gotten them.

I raced over boulders on the banks, trying to keep up with them, urging them to swim to shore as hard as they could. All I could think was that I would have five more days on the river, that we were at least 100 miles in any direction from being able to communicate with the outside world, and that when I finally got to a phone, I'd have to call back home to Minnesota and tell two sets of parents that their sons' bodies were somewhere downriver. Jay made it to shore, and my dreaded phone call was down to one set of parents. But Jay headed back out to help Ricky. Somehow, they were able to get back to the bank before the next rapids. It's hard to scold a couple cocky kids when you're crying.

That evening on the Salmon is stamped on my brain. And it's a perfect example of Luther's view of the human condition. Ricky and Jay did not like our guide's warning words and strictures, and they decided they knew their strength better. They decided to go it on their own. What else would they have done? How could they not have been Ricky and Jay? Those two young men were stuck with their own hubris, their own hormone-filled brains, their own desire to conquer all they surveyed. What Melanchthon was doing in his description of sin in the Augsburg Confession was talking about Ricky and Jay and all of us caught up in the situation we find ourselves in. How you understand free will and sin will make all the difference in whether you come out of the Reformation with Luther or with those who have been in opposing camps for the last 500 years.

When Melanchthon uses words like "innate disease" and "born in sin," it's another way of saying that just by being born a human being, we're stuck on one side of the veil, with the hidden God on the other side. Sin is all about what happens when we try to get at that God: we are bound to react by turning to something else that will do what God won't. The stories of the creation, of Adam and Eve in the Garden of Eden, of the serpent's temptation of Eve in Genesis 3, and of our first parents' rejection of God tell us the same thing using a different angle.

It all begins with, well, the beginning—and especially with how God makes it all happen. Genesis tells us,

> In the beginning God created the heavens and the earth. Now the earth was formless and empty, darkness was over the surface of the deep, and the Spirit of God was hovering over the waters. And God said, "Let there be light," and there was light. God saw that the light was good, and he separated the light from the darkness. God called the light "day," and the darkness he called "night." And there was evening, and there was morning—the first day. (1:1–5 NIV)

God uses a simple, ordinary thing to create something out of nothing (theologians use a Latin phrase: *creatio ex nihilo*). Divine words create the cosmos. When God speaks, stuff happens: light, seas, the moon and stars, and creatures that slither, swim, and fly all appear. Finally, God's words speak you into existence. Those divine words establish a relationship with the creation. Just like when you're angry and say, "I'm going to give her a piece of my mind," God's words in Genesis are an expression—literally God's very being pushed out like breast milk as this new creation in such a way that the whole cosmos exists in and because of God.

The relationship God's Word creates shows up clearly in the phrase delivered by the prophet Jeremiah: "I will be their God, and they will be my people" (Jeremiah 31:33 NIV). God's Word is about God constantly and eternally creating and sustaining that relationship with both you and the whole creation. It is the story of patriarchs, judges, kings, and prophets in the Old Testament. As we will see, it's the story of Jesus. It is the story of Paul and Silas; Peter and Mary Magdalene; Lydia; Dorcas; Augustine and his hovering mother, Monica; the massively embodied Thomas Aquinas; Martin Luther; Dorothy Day; Martin Luther King Jr.; and Johnny Cash. And it is the story of you since your baptism.

But something went wrong when the human creatures that God made for this relationship spurned the intended connection. It goes back to the great chasm between a hidden God and God's human creatures who live in this tangible, earthly realm. In Genesis 2, God puts the man and woman in Eden, smack in the middle of God's delight (which is what the garden's name means). That tells you something about the good pleasure God takes in the creation and God's relationship with it. But God is also aware of the difference between being God and being human. God tells our first parents to eat up; everything in Eden is made to please and sustain. There's only one thing God forbids Adam and Eve to eat: the fruit of the tree of the knowledge of good and evil. In this one rule, God retains all the great *omni*'s that theologians use to describe God: omniscience, omnipresence, and omnipotence. God is all-knowing, all-present, and all-powerful. There are things that remain only in God's job portfolio, ultimate things like life and death, heaven and hell, and here in the garden, the judgment of good and evil. Even God's great promise in Jeremiah we saw above ("I will be their God, and they will be my people") asserts that God will be God. And in the garden, Adam and Eve—and by implication, all their descendants including you—may not cross the line. God tells them his determination to be God and remain God is so great that the consequence of bridging the chasm by eating of the tree will be death.

The problem, of course, is that it is so very hard to trust a God who remains hidden. Sure, God is present in the whole of the creation—God made it, after all—but as we have seen, how are you to find a God secreting himself behind all the masks? We saw that the serpent in the garden zeroed in on that question. The serpent's temptation in Genesis 3 wasn't to hold out some of the tree's juicy fruit for Adam's and Eve's hungry mouths to savor. Instead, the temptation was to not trust the word of a God who would not be seen. The temptation was to think that God isn't good and maybe, just maybe, is holding something back that you want or deserve—something like the knowledge of good and evil or other things that would give you power and control in what seems like a random world and before what seems like an arbitrary God.

When Adam and Eve were tempted, they found it was impossible to avoid sinning because of their misplaced trust. Christian thinkers in the Middle Ages said it is *non posse non peccare*, or "not possible to keep from sinning." This kind of sin is called original sin. Think of it as the Sin (uppercase) that's the origin of all other sins (lowercase)—a condition that makes the rest possible and keeps you from ever being able to avoid them. That is a different way of thinking about sin than you might often hear of. Usually, people talk about sins as bad things you do or good things you avoid doing. We ought to pay attention to those kinds of sins because they have all kinds of consequences for both you and your neighbors in the world. But there is a deeper way to talk about Sin that can lead you to understand yourself *and* your Lord in an equally deep way. Thinking about sins as wrong thoughts and actions comes right out of the story of Adam and Eve and the serpent, but so does thinking about Sin as a condition.

The first way to look at the story is to use the traditional label for it: the Fall. In this way of interpreting the story, Adam and Eve entered into a downward Fall by eating the fruit of the tree of the knowledge of good and evil. Our first parents had an exalted place in the creation. God had given them dominion over all things, after all. But the serpent tempted them to submit to their baser urges. Eating the fruit of the tree was wrong, and they became less than what God had intended them to be. Through their bad actions, they moved down from their exalted place and away from God. If God is spirit and the Edenic couple were flesh, they abandoned the spiritual and the godly, and they attached themselves to the mundane things of the earth—and, as theologians like St. Augustine taught, Adam and Eve were especially moved by their physical urges, including sex. They turned their backs on the ultimate spiritual being and engaged in wrong physical actions. That's lowercase sin— "little *s* sin."

Think of the setup for this story as a great ladder reaching up to God on the top rung. Every creature has its place on the ladder, and to repair the breach with God, our task is to climb up the ladder and become ever more godly and spiritual. In this downward Fall, Adam and Eve climbed down rung after rung, and in every sinful action after that, they moved ever farther down the ladder. If sin is moving away from God and our problem is doing things wrong, then the solution to our sinfulness is to climb back up the ladder. Reversing the downward Fall requires upward striving, spiritual success, more devotion, and endless doses of religion. The way to make things right is to start doing things right. The most important agent in your salvation is you. *You* have to do the work of turning away from your urges, instincts, and inclinations. *You* have to engage in spiritual exercises to counteract your flesh-driven sin. It's a good thing you have Christ on your side, though, because he can show you how to live right. In this way of looking at the story, Jesus' main job is to be a role model, and his death on the cross is all about giving you an example of how to endure hard stuff. Christian life in this scheme follows what Thomas à Kempis called the "Imitation of Christ." A Christian's days, then, are intended to be a constant refrain of "What would Jesus do?" And the power of Christ's death and resurrection becomes an afterthought, if it is thought of at all.

It all hinges on the assumption that you have free will. The Scholastic theology Luther was taught said that you have a spark of goodness left in your fallen, sinful self. The only thing needed is a little oomph from God's grace to fan it into flame. Then you could exert your free will and decide to become the person God made you to be. You could freely opt for God's will, fulfill God's commands, and merit what Christ had done on the cross. The catchphrase of that theology was *facere quod in se est*, or "do what is within you to do." Choose to do your best, and God will do the rest. There were plenty of options for what you could choose: pilgrimages, visiting relics, entering a monastery, or donating some cash to the church's latest fund raiser. The problem for Luther was that the focus remains on you; it all devolves into some moral system where God becomes a divine CPA and Jesus is left out of the equation. In the end, you never turn away from yourself. You always swim across the river and get caught in the current. You always find yourself in the rapids with no way out. The end of the story is always a dead you.

The other way of thinking about what happened in the garden looks at it as an upward Fall. The first question Eve hears when she encounters the serpent has to do with being able to trust God's Word. The serpent reminds her of the strictures against eating the fruit of the tree of the knowledge of good and evil, particularly the warning that eating will bring death. Eve is forced to answer the worst question you could face on this side of the chasm between us and God: Did God really say this? She and the man start wondering if God can really be trusted. Maybe God was lying about dying. Shouldn't they be allowed *everything* in the garden? They deserve it. Why is God keeping something from them? It was not enough for them to be God's human creatures. They wanted more. The serpent's temptation is to point them to the throne of God and get them to think it is empty.

Nature abhors a vacuum, and so, apparently, does the human heart. If we can't see a divine being occupying the throne, we have a perfect candidate for what we think will be the cushy divine chaise longue in the sky. Adam and Eve no sooner hear the serpent's temptation than they plop themselves into God's throne. Instead of turning *away* from godliness and engaging in bad actions and bodily urges like in the downward Fall, Adam and Eve raised themselves to a high position. They put themselves in God's place. In essence, they made themselves their own gods. You could say it another way: Sin is always a disregard for God's Word, for the relationship that God imparts in creating you. This way of looking at your problem as a creature who does not trust God is Sin—"big *S* Sin." It's a condition on whose coat-tails all the "little *s*" sins float into the world. When you think about Sin in this way, it will change who you think Jesus is, what the remedy for your condition is, and what you think the Christian life looks like.

With the upward Fall, God does not fix things by simply demanding that you straighten up and fly right. This way of thinking rejects your free will and assumes instead that you are captive to your own will. Here God recognizes the chasm and your terror of the hidden God and so reveals to you in the person of Jesus exactly what kind of God you have on your hands. All those "little *s*" sins are dealt with at their root when the Word that was the agent of creation at the beginning comes to you in the historical down-to-earth person of Jesus Christ. At the beginning of his gospel, John tags Jesus as the Word: "In the beginning was the Word, and the Word was with God, and the Word was God" (1:1). In Jesus you are given God fully, in the way God wants to be known. Now the Christian life is not about constantly improving your moral backbone, being more frenetic in your religious activity, or becoming less worldly by attaining pure spirituality. Instead, the Christian life is what the old Shaker hymn, "Simple Gifts," says: You "come 'round right" to "live in the valley of love and delight." That involves God bringing you into his divine promise, into the Word, where you can hear exactly what God is up to with you.

We have already heard a bit about the spat between Luther and Erasmus of Rotterdam. In Luther's response to the great humanist, he said that by zeroing in on the matter of free will, Erasmus had understood the essential question at the core of everything: your messed up will. Once you clear up this business of the captive will, everything else will fall in place. In a later treatise, Luther argued that the main task of laypeople in a congregation is to judge doctrine. What he meant is that laypeople need to hold the feet of their pastors to the fire and demand that the clergy get their theological act together. I'd argue that the place to start is to begin listening carefully to how we talk about God, Christ, and the Christian life. Most folks would say the most important thing to listen for in a sermon, for instance, is grace. But grace does not ever truly exist if you have free will. You need to be on guard for any time free will wants to sneak back into the equation.

But if preachers understand Sin and the captive will, then something amazing will happen. When you finally despair of your ability to freely make your future happen, then God can go to town on you with the gospel and make his will come alive in your life. That's when God pulls you down the ladder to where you belong, as a creature who fears, loves, and trusts God, and as one who begins serving your neighbor. When Luther explained the Ten Commandments in the Small Catechism, each of his explanations had two parts. Each commandment means that you "should fear and love God so that . . ." and then continues with what you should and should not do: "We should fear and love God so that we neither despise nor anger our parents and others in authority, but instead honor, serve, obey, love and respect them."[2] The first half of each explanation shows the kinds of things you're bound to do when you place yourself on the divine throne and proclaim yourself your own god. The second half of each explanation describes what you'll look like with faith: You'll trust God to be God. You will be content to remain a human creature. And you will serve your neighbors—other people, other creatures, and the creation itself. In fact, you'll have your petitions in the Lord's Prayer answered and be forgiven when you confess your sins. When you pray "hallowed by thy name, thy kingdom come, thy will be done," God will make you relish those things and turn away from your own name, kingdom, and will. And on Sunday morning, when you declare your captivity and inability to free yourself, it becomes the beginning of a trek into faith that has heaven, the new creation, and the New Jerusalem as its destination.

---

[2] Luther, "Small Catechism," 352.

Chapter 3

Starting with Christ,
the God Who Shows Up

By the time Martin Luther came on the scene in the 16th century, Christian theology in the Western church had been heavily influenced by the ancient Greek philosophy of Aristotle and Plato. Even great theologians like St. Augustine and St. Thomas Aquinas used Greek philosophy as the framework for their thinking about God and human beings.

The late medieval theology Luther was schooled in was largely speculative. Aristotle in ancient Greece wanted to explain everything he encountered in the natural world. He used his powers of observation to figure it all out. By the 13th century, Catholic theologians had rediscovered Aristotle. Thomas Aquinas wanted to do with God what Aristotle had done with the natural world. He tried to use his rational mind to answer every possible question about God. The problem with that approach is something you've already discovered: How can we human beings, who can't observe a hidden God, really know what God is like or whether God looks kindly on us?

Luther argued that we can't really know if a rainbow or a good golf score or kids who turn out are evidence that God is good, because the very same God also sends droughts, forest fires, cancer, enlarged prostates, and every other thing that makes life feel like utter chaos. For Luther, the answer was not to speculate about God but instead to go looking for him where he actually reveals himself—that the place to start in any conversation about God was always Christ himself.

In the Old Testament, God provided the Israelites with the commandments. And he spoke through the prophets. And when the Israelites were faithless, God remained faithful. Even so, those were only the briefest of glimpses behind the divine veil. For Luther, if you want to know who God is, what God is like, and how God regards you, the *only* place to look is the place where God chose to show himself: in the person of Jesus. If you know Jesus, you know God. And the place you get to know Jesus is in the gospels. If we think of the articles of the Augsburg Confession as tools like a screwdriver, crescent wrench, hammer, and vise grip, then Jesus is the box that all our tools come in. All the other things the Augsburg Confession tackles come because Jesus gave them to us or because they're inferences drawn out from who Jesus is.

The Gospel of Mark begins with a big claim about Jesus. He starts with these words: "The beginning of the good news of Jesus Christ the Son of God" (1:1). At first glance, that's a pretty sweet announcement. But when you start digging into Mark's gospel, you'll quickly notice that the truth of the matter is unlike what we might expect from a Jesus who is good news, the Christ, and the Son of God. We might first expect Jesus to be good news for the kind of people American popular culture portrays Christians as: the religious, the moral, the upright, and the hyperspiritual. But those people, the religious leaders in Jerusalem, are the *last* people who want anything to do with the Lord. Their reaction to him isn't adoration or admiration but utter scorn and an underhanded plot to have him arrested and executed. The people who see Jesus as good news, though, are those the religious folks look down their noses at: prostitutes, adulterers, tax collectors, and sinners, including a pagan centurion from Rome, who was the first person to say publicly that "surely this man was the Son of God."

And how about Jesus as Christ? The Greek word *christos* is a translation of the ancient Hebrew word *meshiach*. In English we translate them as "Christ" and "Messiah." They both mean "the anointed king." When Mark calls Jesus "the Christ," he's putting Jesus in line with his ancestor King David. Mark even tells of Jesus the King in a crown and royal robes. Jesus is surely a king who cares for, protects, and provides for his people. But he doesn't function like a powerful descendent of King David, ready to evict the Roman soldiers occupying Judea. Instead, he wears a crown of thorns and takes the cross as his throne. Jesus is an anointed king more like the suffering servant in Isaiah: "He had no form or majesty that we should look at him, nothing in his appearance that we should desire him. He was despised and rejected by others; a man of suffering and acquainted with infirmity" (53:2–3).

As for Jesus as the Son of God, what can we say? This is the Lord who can calm the wind and the waves, cast out demons, give the paralyzed working hamstrings, and heal a woman who has hemorrhaged for a dozen years. But more important, this is a God of *kenosis*. He is the self-emptying God, who on the cross poured out all his divine power and every last ounce of life and breath. Degraded and humiliated, Jesus became the dregs of humanity. Or as Paul says, he who knew no sin became sin for us. We find life in Jesus, who is the God who dies (2 Corinthians 5:21).

Here's what Luther said about Jesus in his explanation of the Second Article of the Apostles' Creed in the Small Catechism:

> I believe that Jesus Christ, true God, begotten of the Father in eternity, and also a true human being, born of the virgin Mary, is my Lord.
>
> He has redeemed me a lost and condemned human being. He has purchased and freed me from all sins, from death, and from the power of the devil, not with silver or gold but with his holy, precious blood and with his innocent suffering and death.
>
> He has done all this in order that I may belong to him, live under him in his kingdom, and serve him in eternal righteousness, innocence, and blessedness, just as he is risen from the dead and lives and rules eternally. This is most certainly true.[1]

That explanation offers plenty that tells you that Jesus as the Christ and the Son of God is good news indeed.

When you start with Christ, your thinking about religion, spirituality, faith, and the church all shift. If we start by looking for evidence in the world around us, we'll find that we stand on shaky ground. No sooner do you experience the beauty of creation than nature slings you a cruel blow. If you take the rainbow as evidence of what God is like, then you also have to take forest fires and floods. It's not that God isn't there. It's just that God is hidden. Luther said that God wears the masks of creation. He's just as likely to show up in disasters as he is in delights. If our conversation about God starts with reason, philosophy, or our own internal senses, we'll be hard put to move out of our own heads. This was one of the main

---

[1] Luther, "Small Catechism," 355.

problems Luther had with the theology he was taught. It was speculation based on philosophy rather than truth revealed by God in Jesus.

But starting with Christ is the faithful move. Instead of asking what God might or might not be like, we look to the places God chooses to show up and show his hand. Then we can start asking questions about what that means for us:

> What does God needing to take on flesh and die on
> the cross mean about who I am?
> What are the criteria that God judges someone by?
> Am I good enough to make it into heaven?
> What's going on in baptism and Communion?
> If Christ saves me because of what he's done and not
> because of what I do, how should I live my life?

The Lenten hymn "O Sacred Head Now Wounded" speaks about the crucified Christ. It was written by Paul Gerhardt in the 17th century. This German pastor faced a storm of troubles in serving his vocation, including the devastation of the Thirty Years' War, eruptions of the black plague, and the deaths of his wives and children. And yet he gives us this sublime hymn that points at this suffering servant whose head is wounded and with grief and shame weighed down. He goes directly to the Lord, a God unlike any god humanity could concoct. And Gerhardt prays that he might only stay connected to this one. In other words, Pastor Gerhardt began with the gift of faith and trust in a savior who looks nothing like a savior. That's what grounded him and gave him hope. And it's what makes the language of justification by faith possible.

Chapter 4

Justification by Faith

Here's a good question that has an unlikely answer: Do sinners get into heaven? Most churchly folks will answer, "Of course!" The problem with our quick answer is that it ignores God's judgment on sin. If sinners get into heaven, then God is a fairly slack divinity when it comes to establishing standards. If it all hinges on God simply being nice and loving toward us like a kindergarten teacher with her charges, then we're engaged in what's called universalism. And worse, we've now made what happened to Jesus on the cross meaningless: if sin isn't a big deal and we get into heaven no matter what, Christ died for nothing.

If we start with Christ as Luther did, then that affects how we talk about how salvation comes about. And the best language for that comes from Paul in Romans and Galatians when he trots out the phrase "justified by faith" (e.g., Romans 3:28, Galatians 3:24). Justification by faith has been called the article by which the church stands or falls. What that means is the entire structure of the church rests on the question of justification. And for Luther, running up against justification changed everything.

In 1545, a couple years before he died, Luther wrote about how everything had shifted 30 years earlier. He remembered his life as a friar in the monastery, teaching the Bible at the University of Wittenberg. He'd been lecturing on Romans to his students, and he remembered hating one passage in particular: "the righteousness of God" in Romans, where Paul says, "The righteous will live by faith" (1:17 NIV).

Luther had been taught the correct interpretation: when you are righteous, you will have faith. First, you become righteous, then you can trust. But Luther began to read that passage in a new way. In Greek, you know how words are related to one another in a sentence by their endings. The ending on the word *God* here means it is in the genitive case. But there are two ways you can read the genitive of a word. *Righteousness of God* can mean "the righteousness that is God's." That's how Luther was taught to read it.

But now he read that genitive ending as *the righteousness* from *God*—that is, "the righteousness God gives." It caused an explosion in him. Where before he virtually hated God for adding the insult of a requirement for righteousness to our lives, which were already riddled with pain and sorrow, now he had a God who gives us his divine righteousness as a gift. Luther started going back through the Bible by memory to see if his new reading would hold water. And he found evidence for it all over the place.

We already encountered the argument Luther had with Erasmus about free will. In that theological kerfuffle, Erasmus dissed Luther for making so many assertions about God. He said you can't do that, because scripture is too murky and obscure to assert things. Luther responded that scripture is completely clear. He could say that because of what he'd experienced himself in his encounter with "the righteousness of God" in Romans. If you get what Paul is up to, then the Bible opens itself up to you, and you can hear God speaking in a way that gives life and faith.

Let's deal quickly with terms. When Luther uses the words *righteousness*, *justification*, and *salvation*, they're virtually synonymous. Anywhere you see one word, you could substitute one of the others and not change the sentence's meaning. If you use a word processing software on your computer, you already know what *justification* means. If you highlight some text in a document and hit Ctrl+L, it will produce a ragged edge along the right margin. But if you hit Ctrl+J, it'll make for a nice even text on the right side of your page. That kind of formatting is called justified text (hence the *J* in your command). The first formatting is unjustified, because the various lines don't meet the mark established by your margins. Justified text, on the other hand, meets the mark of the margin, and it's totally *right*eous, dude.

To be unjustified with God means that we don't meet the mark. We're sinners. And the judgment is in: sinners don't get into heaven. Think of heaven in terms of the relationship established by God's Word in the beginning, the thing that places you within God's delight. As a sinner, you stand outside of God's delight, outside of that intended relationship with God. You've turned your back on that Word. The centerpiece of Lutheran theology is an assertion about how the breach is to be repaired. How can a person who can never meet the intended mark ever get what it promises? The famous Lutheran answer is "justification by faith apart from works of the law."

The language of justification comes out of Paul's letters. It's in both Romans and Galatians. Let's just look at Galatians, because the logic there is a little easier to follow. Paul wrote this letter to people he'd preached to in central Turkey and who had come to faith. After he'd left Galatia, some Christians from Jerusalem came up to make sure everything was in order. They told the Galatians that in order to be followers of Christ they needed to follow the Jewish laws just like Jesus, including being circumcised.

Paul's main theme in his letter to the Galatians is whether you have to do something to be saved. So we have the question, How do we meet the mark established by God? In Galatians, Paul lays it out: "We ourselves are Jews by birth and not Gentile sinners; yet we know that a person is justified not by the works of the law but through faith in Jesus Christ" (2:15–16). He reminds the Galatians that he's Jewish, which means he's circumcised and follows the other Jewish religious laws like not eating shellfish and pork, not wearing two different kinds of fabric, and so on. But he says even observant Jews, such as himself, who believe in Christ know that justification and salvation don't happen on account of adhering to any laws. He argues that your salvation happens by believing that Christ has taken care of it, regardless of whether you live as a Jew, following their customs and rules or not.

Luther used two pairs of words that can help us understand what's going here: active and passive righteousness. *Active righteousness* is the goodness that comes about because of what we do. This is the righteousness that Luther struggled with in the medieval interpretation of the phrase "the righteousness of God." And given what we know about our Sin (with a capital *S*) and our captive will, we know exactly how far that will get us. There's no amount of work we can do to establish enough righteousness to be accepted by God, because everything we do will always be clouded over by our captive will, our Sin, our adoration of ourselves.

Passive righteousness, though, is a righteousness that is foreign to you. It's a righteousness that comes apart from anything you do. It's given to you, placed in you, without your having done a lick of work to make it happen. Such righteousness comes as a gift. Paul reminded the newbie Christians that their salvation doesn't come by their own actions or willpower. Instead, it arrives from the outside. We could say it comes from God's eternal future. The technical theological way to say this is that righteousness is *imputed*. It's credited to your account. It's passive, because you can't do anything to get it. You can only *believe* that it has been given to you.

Paul's opponents in Galatia had argued that the new believers there who had converted from paganism must submit to Jewish law to become righteous. Paul acknowledged Jewish law earlier, but he argued here that from the beginning the chosenness of the Jews wasn't because they followed laws. The Jews looked back to Abraham as their father in the faith, and they knew that God didn't call him righteous because of what he did but because he trusted. And Paul went further, saying that Abraham's righteousness was a foreshadowing of what the Galatians had now been given in Christ, in whom they had come to believe.

In his defense of the Wittenberg teaching before the officials of the Holy Roman Empire and of the Roman church at the Diet of Augsburg in 1530, Philip Melanchthon professed this central teaching:

> [Our churches] teach that human beings cannot be justified before God by their own powers, merits, or works. But they are justified as a gift on account of Christ's sake through faith when they believe that they are received into grace and that their sins are forgiven on account of Christ, who by his death made satisfaction for our sins. God reckons this faith as righteousness.[1]

The Latin phrase for "before God" in the middle of the first line is *coram deo*. Melanchthon is talking about our standing before God—that is, whether we meet the mark. He says, "This faith [that is, *saving* faith] God imputes for

---

[1] Melanchthon, "Augsburg Confession," 39, 41.

righteousness *coram deo*." When we talked about the captive will in an earlier chapter, we saw that though we can make choices in the things beneath us, we can't in regard to the things above us. Those things above us are *coram deo*. In God's sight, *coram deo*, we're justified. But in the things beneath us, until our dying breath we remain sinners. Luther had a phrase for that: *simul iustus et peccator*—simultaneously justified and sinful.

There's a great story in Mark's gospel that shows how this works:

> When they came to the disciples, they saw a great crowd around them, and some scribes arguing with them. When the whole crowd saw him, they were immediately overcome with awe, and they ran forward to greet him. He asked them, "What are you arguing about with them?" Someone from the crowd answered him, "Teacher, I brought you my son; he has a spirit that makes him unable to speak; and whenever it seizes him, it dashes him down; and he foams and grinds his teeth and becomes rigid; and I asked your disciples to cast it out, but they could not do so." He answered them, "You faithless generation, how much longer must I be among you? How much longer must I put up with you? Bring him to me." And they brought the boy to him. When the spirit saw him, immediately it convulsed the boy, and he fell on the ground and rolled about, foaming at the mouth. Jesus asked the father, "How long has this been happening to him?" And he said, "From childhood. It has often cast him into the fire and into the water, to destroy him; but if you are able to do anything, have pity on us and help us." Jesus said to him, "If you are able!—All things can be done for the one who believes." Immediately the father of the child cried out, "I believe; help my unbelief!" When Jesus saw that a crowd came running together, he rebuked the unclean spirit, saying to it, "You spirit that keeps this boy from speaking and

hearing, I command you, come out of him, and never enter him again!" After crying out and convulsing him terribly, it came out, and the boy was like a corpse, so that most of them said, "He is dead." But Jesus took him by the hand and lifted him up, and he was able to stand. (9:14–27)

The father's answer to Jesus is *simul iustus et peccator*: "I believe and don't believe at the same time. I can't make it work. Help me." If justification by faith apart from works of the law is true, then our situation is dire and urgent. We need saving faith. Our question has to be, "How can I get me some of that good stuff?" In order to find it, you'll need to know where God wants to be found.

Chapter 5

Delivering the Goods

This might be a good spot to do a quick review of the Articles of the Augsburg Confession we've taken up so far. Article I is about almighty God, whom we talked about as the hidden God. Article II is about Sin, our constant penchant to trust ourselves rather than God. Article III is about the revealed God in the person of Jesus Christ. Article IV is about how we're justified or saved by faith rather than by good works, good intentions, or good hair. Notice that so far, we have two articles about who God is and what God does. And we have two articles that focus on what happens to human beings: how we sin and how we're saved by Jesus. If Article I is about God the Father and Article III is about God the Son, we might expect that the next article is going to be about the Holy Spirit. It is, but not in the way you expected.

Article V is about the office of preaching, but I think Philip Melanchthon, the author of the Augsburg Confession, is up to something here. And we're also right to think this article is about the Holy Spirit. Look at what the article says.

> To obtain such faith God instituted the office of preaching, giving the gospel and the sacraments. Through these, as through means, he gives the Holy Spirit who produces faith, where and when he wills, in those who hear the gospel. It teaches that we have a gracious God, not through our merit but through Christ's merit, when we so believe. Condemned are the Anabaptists and others who teach that we obtain the Holy Spirit without the external word of the gospel through our own preparation, thoughts, and works.[1]

Let's take this piece by piece and see if I can't show you why this is my favorite article. I like it even better than the famous article about justification by faith.

"To obtain such faith": this phrase points backward to Article IV that says we're justified—that is, we're saved from our sin (Article II) by God (Article I), not by doing good works or engaging in religious activities, but solely by faith. We're justified by trusting that Christ has taken it all on and gives us salvation freely and graciously (Article III). What you're about to get is the *how*, as in "How is God ever going to get me to trust so fully that he truly becomes my God?"

Notice, too, who's obtaining this faith. We could easily think we get faith by deciding to have faith. But that turns faith into another dreary good work done under obligation or threat of hell. What if it's God doing the obtaining? In other words, in order to produce faith in us, this is what God does. That keeps things in line with what we know from Romans: "Faith comes from what is heard, and what is heard comes through the word of Christ" (10:17). Faith comes to you from outside yourself. It's not something that you can whip up.

In 1977, a week after my high school graduation I started working at Outlaw Ranch, one of our Bible camps in

---

[1] Melanchthon, "Augsburg Confession," 40.

the Black Hills in South Dakota. There were a couple charismatic Lutherans on staff whom I admired. When I started at
Augustana College in the fall, one of them, named Becky was
also a student there. I thought the whole charismatic thing
sounded cool, so I prayed and prayed and prayed for the gift
of the Spirit. I wanted God to grab me and give me the ability
to speak in tongues. The only tongue I got was the one that
savored the cheeseburgers and fries in the Viking Huddle a
little too much. Otherwise I was stuck with the utterly mundane ability to speak my native prairie-billy English from
western South Dakota and some high school German.

Faith, like its partners hope and love in 1 Corinthians
13:13, is something that happens to you. The day I met my
wife on January 1, 1990, I didn't wake up and think, "This is
a good day to fall in love. I think I'll try that this afternoon."
No, what happened is that she showed up at our pastors'
house for a Rose Bowl watching party, and I fell hard. I didn't
expect it, and I didn't have to try to make it happen. Hope,
too, is something given to you by a trustworthy promise. So
faith is obtained. God makes it happen.

Now Melanchthon tells you about the vehicle God uses
to deliver it to you. Naturally if something is being delivered,
you need a FedEx truck. Think about the FedEx logo, which
I think is the best-designed logo in the world. What sits in
between the *E* and the *X*? That's right. It's an arrow. Every
time you see a FedEx truck, you can remember that faith is
like an arrow being shot into you. The FedEx truck that God
uses to bring you faith is *the office of preaching* or *the office of
ministry*. Note to whom this office belongs: it's *God's* office.
It's wrong for pastors to talk about *their* ministry, because it's
God's ministry. And if the office of preaching is the vehicle,
who brings the goods to you? It's not the pastor. It's the Holy
Spirit who steps out of the truck, package in hand.

For Melanchthon, the office of preaching consists of two
things: the gospel and the sacraments. This is all about the

Word of God. The gospel is the proclaimed Word, both law and gospel, that does what God declares in Deuteronomy: "See now that I, even I, am he; there is no god besides me. I kill and I make alive; I wound and I heal; and no one can deliver from my hand" (32:39). When we sing "A Mighty Fortress Is Our God," we sing "one little word subdues him." The "him" there is the devil. For Martin Luther, there's only one thing powerful enough to deliver you from sin, death, and the devil. And that is the Word of God. At the end of the cosmic battle between good and evil in John's vision in Revelation, a pale rider comes in on a white horse to finish all our evil enemies. John says, "From his mouth comes a sharp sword with which to strike down the nations, and he will rule them with a rod of iron; he will tread the wine press of the fury of the wrath of God the Almighty" (19:15). Why a sword in his mouth? It's because Jesus' only weapon is the Word of God, which has been present from the very first moment of creation.

Just as when we talk about Christ "emptying himself," the Word of God is God pushing all divinity out from himself in order to create and sustain every living thing. It's God's electing Word, as God chose Abraham and his progeny to be blessed to provide God's blessing to the world. It's the prophetic Word that held a mirror up to the Israelites' faithlessness and that also held them close in the midst of their captivity in Babylon. And above all, it's the Word of promise present in the person of Jesus Christ declaring the advent of the kingdom of God, present in his promise to the thief on the cross next to his, present in the angel within the tomb's depths saying to the grieving women come to dress the Lord's limp body, "He is risen from the dead."

The Word is, thus, first a proclaimed Word, declared to sinners and to the ungodly and to spiritual layabouts like me. In order to create faith, what's needed is a preacher to speak it into you. This proclaimed Word doesn't just come from the pulpit; it also comes in the announcement of absolution. And it comes in the mutual conversation and consolation of the saints, whenever two or more are gathered in Christ's name speaking the good news that travels from one set of lips to another set of ears. There's a physical version of the Word as well, when the Word attaches itself to physical elements—to water in baptism and to bread and wine in the Lord's Supper. All these little words subdue what is anti-Christ—that is, what seeks to prevent faith. You may have spotted something missing so far: nowhere does Article V say anything about pastors. That's because God is kind of promiscuous in his choice of proclamatory partners. He'll use just about anybody to get the cardboard Amazon box full of Christ's benefits to your front porch, even an annoying 10-year-old sister.

I grew up in Sturgis, South Dakota. You may have heard of it. That's the place with all the motorcycles. To say more about my experience with our annual rally and its hundreds of thousands of leather-clad and unclad participants wouldn't be appropriate. But when I was a kid, Sturgis was a lovely place. We lived on the outskirts of town in a little eight-wide trailer house. We were part of the tiny house movement before anyone knew there was such a thing.

One summer morning when I was six or seven, my older sister Gine and I were running through the sprinkler to stay cool. We were kids who were always singing. Here, too, it was sprinkler spritzing and singing songs. But we didn't sing your normal kids' ditties like "London Bridge" or "This Old Man" or "B-I-N-G-O." My sister had gone to church kindergarten where they taught the kids hymns like "My Faith Looks Up to Thee" and "Beau*teef*ul Savior." At some point during the singing and splashing, my sister decided it was time to go over to the corner of the yard and play school at the picnic table we had in the shade. I wanted none of that, and because I knew who always got to play teacher, I headed inside for a big glass of Kool-Aid in a 1960s aluminum glass.

As I came around the front of the trailer, I grabbed hold
of the hitch to swing around it like any active kid would. And
it was like the trailer house was sucking me into itself. You
know what it's like when you get a shock from a bad outlet?
That's what it was like. But the buzzing didn't stop. If I used
all my strength I could pull one hand away, but the other
wouldn't come loose. I yelled to my sister for help as loud as
I could, but she couldn't hear me. I was being electrocuted,
and the electricity was zapping the strength from my voice.
It all seemed like it was happening in slow motion. But it
ended as quickly as it began. My sister, who was safe because
she was wearing leather-soled sandals, grabbed my arm to
make me stop what she thought was my messing around.
And she pulled me away from being as good as dead. As
she dragged me away from the killing electrical field, my
beloved sister was still singing. The words coming off her
lips were the sweetest announcement of mercy in the shape
of another hymn: "I know that my Redeemer lives: What joy
that blest assurance gives! He lives, he lives, who once was
dead; He lives, my everlasting head!"[2]

Somehow in that moment, something significant happened. A kid's electrocution became a sermon on his baptism.
As good as dead, I had been handed back my life. And it
became linked with the fact that Jesus himself lay dead and
now lives. My life was no longer my own. Every minute I've
lived since 1966, every breath I've drawn into my lungs, has
come on account of someone else's actions. I couldn't breathe
or pull my other hand away from that hitch to save my life.
But death had no power over my sister that day. I was literally
grounded in death and given new life. That's where we always
have to begin when we're talking about our lives as Christians:
with the realization and confession that none of this—*none* of

    [2] Samuel Medley, "I Know That My Redeemer Lives!," in *Lutheran Book of Wor-
ship* (Minneapolis: Augsburg, 1978), hymn 352.

this—happened because of something *we* did or even had the possibility of doing. It all happened because of Christ.

In 1518, Martin Luther wrote a piece for a gathering of his fellow Augustinian friars called the Heidelberg Disputation. In it, he was throwing shade at people who said we could use our free will to choose to be saved. Luther pushed back against that thinking, saying that if you could bend your will to decide to be the person God wanted you to be, then we wouldn't have needed what Christ did on the cross. And saying that was true meant you were dissing Jesus. Then Luther went on to say a curious thing: "It is certain that one must completely despair of oneself in order to be made fit to receive the grace of Christ."[3] Another way of saying that is "As long as you think you have something to contribute to your salvation or bring to God, you don't get it yet."

This can help us in the important task of finding what's true and pure in any preaching—that is, in asking whether the office of preaching is happening. Judging a sermon, for the most part, is impossible. That's because God's Word comes to each person differently. Because our hearts exist with varying levels of despair and need for what Jesus has come to deliver, the first move to make in judging the office of preaching lies in looking at your own heart. Ask, "Has this sermon left me some wiggle room? Has this sermon allowed me to imagine I can sustain my own future? Has this sermon left my heart intact?"

Next, if preaching has pulled the pool cue out of your hands, then you need to ask who's going to break what's been racked up in order to start the game of getting us billiard balls safe and secure into the pockets of the table. True preaching insists that it's all in Christ's hands. In my seminary days, one of my preaching professors, Gracia Grindal, used to ask, "Did Christ have to die for this sermon to be preached?" It's

---

[3] Martin Luther, "Heidelberg Disputation," in *The Annotated Luther: The Roots of Reform*, trans. Timothy J. Wengert (Minneapolis: Fortress, 2015), 1:83.

another way of asking whether the burden of your salvation is securely on Jesus, whether the proclamation has tucked you into the spear wound in Jesus' side.

Finally, any preaching is a true and holy Word and part of God's office if it's for you. Melanchthon says the Holy Spirit "produces faith, where and when he wills, in those who hear the gospel" and "when we believe" that it's for us. The office of preaching is "for you" when it takes seriously your brokenness, shame, and guilt; your wake of failures; and the burden of regrets and mistakes you bear each day. That means it has to deal with you as a real sinner and not a sham sinner.

Or to go back to my electrocution, the office of preaching is truly about the resurrection of the dead. It grabs hold of you when you're dying or have one foot in the grave or are even lying dead and cold in the ground (or nice and warm in a crematorium). And it yanks you into new life. Another of my teachers, Gerhard Forde, once wrote a book about justification by faith. Its subtitle was *A Matter of Death and Life*.[4] The office of preaching is serious business, because it's about God breaking in from eternity to pitch a tent in your messy existence. It's about ultimate things rather than garbage like prosperity, popularity, PowerPoint slides, or other penultimate matters. It's about no less than God, who declares he's a jealous God, having you absolutely to himself. And it's about the Lord Jesus Christ, who gets the job done. Amen.

---

[4] Gerhard O. Forde, *Justification by Faith: A Matter of Death and Life* (Philadelphia: Fortress, 1982).

Chapter 6

Being Made New

I learned about sheep ranching through the bustle of lambing season at the 2-Lazy J Ranch, my grandparent's spread in western South Dakota. In March of each year, sheep ranchers would bring in the sheep for lambing season, and they'd have a shed set aside for the bum lambs. Those lambs were on the verge of death with no future at all. The bum lambs were those whose ewes had died lambing or who were the runt in a set of triplets. Either because there was no mother to feed them or because they'd be pushed away by the other two triplets, they'd wind up starving. The bum lambs have nothing but death ahead of them.

In another shed, my grandpa Buster and uncle Bobby would put the expectant ewes in pens full of straw, out of the cold and the muck of an early spring barnyard. Every once in a while, a ewe would give birth to a stillborn lamb or one so sickly that it quickly died, and we Joneses had to deal with a different situation: a ewe with an udder full of milk but no lamb to suckle. What's a smart rancher to do? Time for an ovine hookup: give a stranded and starving bum lamb to the ewe to raise.

But one whiff of the bum lamb would tell the ewe that this wasn't hers. The smell was all wrong, and she wouldn't let the lamb near her teats. The hungry bum lamb would be on the receiving end of a back hoof. My grandpa and uncle would be forced to jacket the bum lamb. They'd slit the ewe's dead lamb's underbelly from jawbone to anus and slice the pelt off. Then they'd drape the skin on the bum lamb, secure it with some baling twine, and set it before the ewe. Now the bum lamb smelled like the ewe's own dead lamb, and she'd take it on as her own.

In the last chapter, we looked at Article V on the office of preaching. We saw that the essential piece for salvation for Philip Melanchthon and Martin Luther was that Christ is delivered through preaching. In the proclaimed Word and the visible Word in the sacraments, the announcement of forgiveness for the ungodly is declared in the name of Christ. Where that Word brings faith, we experience what Luther called "the happy exchange." In other words, we bum lambs who are dead in sin are given the place of the Lamb of God, who was slain from the foundation of the world. Paul says in Colossians, "For you have died, and your life is hidden with Christ in God" (3:3).

Now we have in front of us Article VI of the Augsburg Confession, on the new obedience. We need to ask what it means for that newly jacketed lamb to wear Jesus' pelt and live not in the bum lamb shed but in the pasture with the herd. Article VI says this:

> Likewise, they teach that this faith is bound to yield good fruits and that it ought to do good works commanded by God on account of God's will and not so that we may trust in these works to merit justification before God. For forgiveness of sins and justification are taken hold of by faith, as the saying of Christ also testifies [Luke 17:10]: "When you have done all [things] . . . say, 'We are worthless slaves.'" The

authors of the ancient church teach the same. For Ambrose says, "It is established by God that whoever believes in Christ shall be saved without work, by faith alone, receiving the forgiveness of sins as a gift."[1]

Luther and his fellow Reformers were often and unjustly accused of teaching and preaching in such a way that it allowed for a moral free-for-all. If faith didn't need to be proved in acts of charity or made visible by amending your immoral life, then you could just do whatever you want. The result would be libertinism and licentiousness. The downhill slide would begin with not going to church, and we'd soon wind up with co-ed naked barbecues, dogs marrying cats, and people voting for the opposing political party. That's anarchy, and it certainly isn't in God's plan.

But that wasn't at all what the Reformers imagined that justification by faith alone would lead to. For Luther, a justifying and saving faith was created by the preaching of the gospel which would then result in a new life of obedience to God's will. In Galatians, Paul says, "The fruit of the Spirit is love, joy, peace, patience, kindness, generosity, faithfulness, gentleness, and self-control" (5:22–23). Notice that each of Paul's fruits of the Spirit is outwardly directed. It involves a turn *away* from remaining *incurvatus in se*—being curved in on yourself. Earlier in Galatians, Paul provides a different list of behaviors that grow from unfaith or what he calls "the flesh": "Now the works of the flesh are obvious: fornication, impurity, licentiousness, idolatry, sorcery, enmities, strife, jealousy, anger, quarrels, dissensions, factions, envy, drunkenness, carousing, and things like these" (5:18–21). These kinds of behaviors have an anti-Christ focus. Instead of being drawn away from yourself to serve others, they

---

[1] Melanchthon, "Augsburg Confession," 41.

insist that yes, there is an *I* in team and in every other possible human activity. Here's what Luther said about it in his Romans lectures: "Our nature has been so deeply curved in upon itself [*incurvatus in se*] because of the viciousness of original sin that it not only turns the finest gifts of God in upon itself and enjoys them (as is evident in the case of legalists and hypocrites), indeed, it even uses God Himself to achieve these aims, but it also seems to be ignorant of this very fact, that in acting so iniquitously, so perversely, and in such a depraved way, it is even seeking God for its own sake."[2]

We know from what has come before in the Augsburg Confession that becoming a new, faithful, and obedient person taken up by God's Spirit isn't something we're capable of achieving. Good works won't do the trick. In fact, attempting to log a bunch of good works in your God diary as evidence of your goodness actually works against you. Any attempt to add something—no matter how good, right, and noble—to what Christ has done for you on the cross results not in greater salvation but in increasing distance from God and, ultimately, to condemnation. In his letter to the Galatians, Paul does a bit of theological algebra. After Paul had preached to the pagan converts in central Turkey and then continued on his missionary journey, the believers in Galatia were visited by Christians from Jerusalem bent on assessing the damage of Paul's preaching. As I mentioned earlier, these folks told the converts in Galatia that being a true Christian meant observing all the Jewish laws and performing all the proper religious rituals, from not eating shellfish to not wearing two kinds of fabrics. The main ritual in question, though, was circumcision: Was altered junk required of the new male believers in Galatia for a Christian

---

[2] Martin Luther, "Lectures on Romans," in *Luther's Works* (St. Louis: Concordia, 1972), 25:291.

life, and what about every other law that appears in the scriptures?

Paul heard about the issue and wrote back in a huff. He accused the Galatians of having been bewitched. He was so angry that he said he wished the people from Jerusalem who demanded circumcision would just castrate themselves (5:12). Paul's main point, though, was that faith in Christ is enough. The equation works like this:

trusting Jesus + x = salvation.

For Paul, the horror of Jesus' crucifixion and death are proof positive that our ability to fix ourselves must have bottomed out for this kind of drastic measure to be called for. Not a single good work, nor even a raft of them, was enough. Thus Christ took it all on, and his death *is* enough. That means that in our equation, the x variable isn't variable at all. It can only ever be zero.

But if obedience in the form of good works can't give you any help in the face of sin, and if they don't do you any good in your final judgment, then why bother doing good works? In his treatise "On the Freedom of a Christian," Luther says there are two reasons to do good works. The first is that your neighbor needs your good works. God is so self-contained, that no good works need to be aimed God's way. Jesus fulfilled the requirements. He is "the end of the law." Good works that are looking for some salvation in return are superfluous at best and, at worst, are a sign that you don't much trust what Jesus did on Golgotha. But your neighbors do indeed have a great need for your service and vocation. I need immigrant farmworkers who pick cabbages and grapes in California that'll become my sauerkraut and cabernet. I need slaughterhouse kill floor knife-wielders for the pork chop on my plate. I need Urbandale water utility guys who see to it that I have drinking water that is both fresh and clean. I need pastors who serve by putting their personal wisdom aside and give me a pure absolution instead. I need a wife who comforts and cares for me and who pays the bills, because I'm constitutionally unable to manage household finances. I need fellow drivers who don't plow through a four-way stop but take turns instead. I need fellow voters who approach the polling place with the seriousness of mind that representative democracy demands and who will work to elect leaders with vision and hope. As a professor, I need a department chair whose industry and scholarship are a model that pulls me out of inertia and complacency.

The second reason to do good works is that the old person in me, the guy who's curved in on himself, hates doing good works. In *Freedom of a Christian*, Luther put it this way: "The human creature cannot be idle because of the demands of its body, and because of the body, it attempts to do many good things to bring it under control."[3] Luther's assumption is that we're like addicts working a program of sobriety. The first step in Alcoholics Anonymous is this: "We admitted we were powerless over alcohol—that our lives had become unmanageable."[4] For Luther, we do good works in order to discipline the unmanageable sinner inside us. We can't create the new person of faith (remember: the Spirit does that with the office of preaching). But where faith exists, we'll see ever more clearly how we don't do what we should and in turn do what we shouldn't. When faith arises, we grab hold of opportunities to make the sinner in us do what it hates—that is, think about others and serve their needs before our own.

---

[3]   Martin Luther, "Freedom of a Christian," in *Annotated Luther*, 1:512.

[4]   "The Twelve Steps of Alcoholics Anonymous," PDF available at "What Is A.A.?," Alcoholics Anonymous official website, accessed June 22, 2020, https://www.aa.org/pages/en_US/what-is-aa.

This is why Jesus teaches us to pray *counter* to ourselves in the first three petitions of the Lord's Prayer: hallowed be *thy* name, *thy* kingdom come, *thy* will be done. To pray the Lord's Prayer and mean what it says is no easy thing. When have you ever actually prayed fully trusting God; turning over your own name, kingdom, and will; and calling on the Lord without reserving some iota of control for yourself? I'd argue that the only time it happens is when the words of "A Mighty Fortress Is Our God" come crashing into our reality: "Were they to take our house, goods, honor, child, or spouse, though life be wrenched away, they cannot win the day." We come closest to perfect obedience, to the new obedience of faith, when our carefully constructed house of cards comes crashing down.

Our litany of disasters is long and full of sorrow. Losing a job and, worse, not landing a new one. A miscarriage, or a third or fourth one. The words *cancer* and *malignant* spoken in the same sentence. The sudden death of a spouse, or his or her long, lingering, and painful passing into the dying of the light—not to mention the drone of too many days in a house emptied of that loved one's bodily presence. These are the times when our power and control are snatched away. They're the life passages when my wife, Mary, and I have clung to each other in bed after the lights have been turned out and our prayers have come in the form of tears, or what Paul calls the Spirit's pleading with sighs too deep for words.

The first obedience, and truly the only real obedience to God, doesn't happen by hewing to some moral code or ethical system. True obedience comes with obeying the First Commandment, that we should fear, love, and trust God above everything else. Suffering, then, is the most fertile ground for obedience. It is the place where, having lost your control and power, you can get the clearest glimpse of what Christ has promised. You'll never understand what it means for the first to be last and the last first until you can cry out, "I've fallen and I can't get up." You cannot know the blessedness of the Beatitudes unless you are one who mourns or is poor in spirit or hunger and thirst for righteousness. Luther used an untranslatable German word to describe this *status teribillissimus*, the most terrible state of affairs. Luther's word was *Anfechtung*. It means trouble, turmoil, temptation, dispute, terror, affliction, and testing—in other words, when you're the mouse and the world is a boa constrictor—all rolled up in one handy word. Late in his life, Luther wrote a piece called "On the Councils and the Church," where he gave a list of seven marks of the church—that is, the seven things by which you can spot the church. All the usual suspects are there: the Word of God, baptism and the Lord's Supper, people called to deliver the public proclamation of the gospel, and worship. But Luther ended his list with suffering as a distinct mark of the church. You yourself will be marked as a part of the church whenever you possess Christ's cross in your sufferings and losses.

Now that we've got the idea of our own crosses seeping into our definition of both our obedience and the church, we'll be well on our way to understanding how the church that is the body of Christ is made manifest in the world.

Chapter 7

The Church? I Don't Even Know What the Church Is Anymore

In political reporting, pundits and talking heads like to ferret out the various causes for voters' choices and election results. And we've heard concerns about the hacking of our system by foreign agents, big money, and social media. But now, as we look at Articles VII and VIII of the Augsburg Confession and what they say about the church, we encounter a much older version of election hacking. Philip Melanchthon, who drafted the Augsburg Confession, pulled the language about the church from the works of his colleague Martin Luther at the University of Wittenberg. Luther regarded the question of the church as an election issue.

As we've moved through the Augsburg Confession, we've seen that God saves us from our sin by creating faith and trust in Jesus as the one who brings righteousness before God, bearing the full burden for it on the cross. (That was Article IV.) The arrival of such faith comes when the Holy Spirit brings the gospel to sinners when and where it pleases. (That's Article V on the office of preaching.) Luther called that process "election." It's all about God's choice. The way God works his electing in the world is to send a preacher. The goal of these two articles is to see to it that God's election doesn't get hacked.

The hacking of God's electing work happens in a way not unlike what we've seen Russian GRU operatives do with social media in intruding on other countries' political activities. Facebook, for instance, gets flooded with incendiary messages intended to get you to think ill of one candidate or party or another. The hacking of God's election comes when the world, the devil, and my sinful self get me to think that I can't count on God's promises in Jesus. Divine election hacking happens with the proposal that God's Word is irrelevant. This little Word that Luther's hymn says subdues the enemies of the gospel comes to be seen as powerless, weak, and impotent. Jesus is not enough, and something needs to be added to the cross.

Usually what gets added is a moral program, a social benefit, or a political movement that the hackers in this election say is really worth your time. The opponents to the Word move in from both the left and the right, from both liberal mainline Christianity and conservative evangelicalism. We get divided into camps either behind a therapeutic moral deism that advocates for social reform, a focus on reparations for victims, and liberal political programs on the one hand or behind a certain kind of fundamentalism and legalism that would embed a list of conservative religious and social values into the structure of society by means of legislation and make our land Christian again. Or there's a third way that's called the "prosperity gospel," which ignores the other hackers and simply treats God as a weak-kneed divinity who can be swayed by your devotion and grant you a perfect life. All these hackers use the tools of popular culture to hook people and reel them in. They play on your desire to fit in, to be regarded as somebody, to hang with the beautiful and powerful, and at the very least to have some measure of control over your future days in this life and over God's ultimate thumbs-up or thumbs-down on the last day.

What's missing from this picture? At best, these hackers want you to serve many noble causes and not-so-random acts of kindness that make the world a better or more moral place. But like Russian operatives, the result is always that you take your eye off the ball to serve your own autonomy. Your attention is pulled away from the one single thing you need for your salvation, the one thing that is required for the existence of the church. What's missing from this picture is Jesus Christ, and him crucified.

A little less than a decade after the Diet of Augsburg and after lots of wrangling in Rome about whether, when, and where to have churchwide council to settle the Reformation uproar, Luther took up the issue again. Earlier we saw a bit of his response in the treatise "On the Councils and the Church" and its list of what he called the "seven marks of the church"—that is, the seven signs by which you can determine if you're seeing Christ's church: the Word of God, baptism, the Lord's Supper, forgiving and retaining sins, people called to deliver the public proclamation of the gospel, worship, and suffering. We can get a clearer sense of Luther's list if we remember what he said about individual Christians in "Freedom of a Christian." He said that each of us has two selves inside us: the old, outer person of the flesh and the new, inner person of the Spirit. The old person who lacks faith relies on works to earn salvation, disregards the Word, and seeks to manage life through relentless activity (and sometimes quits caring altogether). But the new person of faith relies solely on Christ and can be spotted by bearing the fruit of the Spirit (love, joy, peace, patience, kindness, goodness, faithfulness, gentleness, and self-control). In the same way, there's an outer church and an inner church.

The outer church is defined by structures, buildings, hierarchies, legal matters, and all sorts of metrics by which we can check on our religious progress. There's the outer church you may be a member of: an institution with a physical place whose door you enter for Sunday worship. That church has a building, it has a church council, it has stuff that fills offices and classrooms and kitchens that are used in carrying out the church's work. You have people on staff and under call. You might have a nursery with a handy machine that connects parents' code numbers with the children involved in Sunday school, or youth and family ministries, and there may be procedures for doing background checks on people who lead those kids. What's more, every congregation has a constitution and bylaws in order to operate legally.

But in the inner church, the one thing that prevails is the gospel of Jesus Christ. That inner church is something we see through a glass dimly. It's barely visible, because it exists in the moment between when the promise of the gospel is delivered and when the Spirit creates a trusting heart in you. The inner church is what exists throughout time wherever and whenever the promise is delivered. That's why the church is catholic—lowercase—and why Melanchthon defined the church as the assembly (*ecclesia* not *communio*) of believers around Word and sacrament. *Church* is a verb. It's something that is done by the Holy Spirit. In a way, Melanchthon might have been wiser to put these two articles between the one on preaching and the one on the new obedience.

The church is like brain chemistry. When we speak, think, and move, we have electrical impulses that travel along neurons. When the electrical jolt gets to the end of a neuron, it faces a gap that it moves across to get to what's next. That gap is a *synapse*. The inner church exists in the gap where all leaps of faith happen, where the move from the old person to the new person takes us from unfaith to faith.

Here's what these two articles say: Article VII is concerned with defining the church, and Article VIII speaks about the people within the church. Article VII, on the church, states,

> They teach that one holy church will remain forever. The church is the assembly of saints in which the gospel is taught purely and the sacraments are administered rightly. And it is enough for the true unity of the church to agree concerning the teaching of the gospel and the administration of the sacraments. It is not necessary that human traditions, rites, or ceremonies instituted by human beings be alike everywhere.[1]

The church is what *God* is doing in our midst, but Article VIII—which asks, "What is the church?"—looks at it from our vantage point:

> Although the church is, properly speaking, the assembly of saints and those who truly believe, nevertheless, because in this life many hypocrites and evil people are mixed in with them, a person may use the sacraments even when they are administered by evil people. . . . Both the sacraments and the Word are efficacious because of the ordinance and command of Christ, even when offered by evil people.[2]

The church, then, is where the goods are delivered and the Spirit's impulse brings people to faith so that they grab hold of Christ's benefits of forgiveness of sin, life, and salvation.

---

[1] Melanchthon, "Augsburg Confession," 43.

[2] Ibid.

If the church is inner and outer, it's because the people assembled there are inner and outer (hence Article VIII). It was an offense to the Reformers' opponents that anyone could consider anything less than absolute religious purity as acceptable. Among those people, both the Roman church on the right and the enthusiasts on the left wanted to make the inner church visible. Luther's Roman antagonists wanted a church bound to the hierarchy and papacy. The enthusiasts wanted a church that didn't involve mediated promises but instead an immediate and measurable display of spiritual gifts. Thus a Roman view of baptism regarded a baptized life as being proved in participation in the Mass and in acts of charity. And the Anabaptists said being a baptized Christian meant having a seal on your prior decision for Christ and then embarking on a new born-again life of moral renewal. All those things can be really good things for Christians to be involved in, but they're *not* the church. If there's any place for those things, they belong back with Article VI on the new obedience. When the church engages in charitable works, advocacy, or politics, it is only via individual believers living their vocation and being urged on by the Holy Spirit.

What the church *does* get to assert is the universal truth that *all* have sinned and fallen short of the glory of God. *All* need the mercy of Immanuel, God made flesh in the person of Jesus Christ. And the way they get it is via election—that is, by means of mercy announced to the ungodly in the name of Christ. Agree with that and we'll have the unity Christ prays for in John 17. In the 1990s, an ecumenical agreement between the Evangelical Lutheran Church in America and the Episcopal Church USA, "Called to Common Mission," required an outer-church indicator called the historic epis-copate. It insisted first that both churches' bishops have hands laid on them by other bishops who were ordained by someone who was ordained by someone who was ordained by someone in a trail that goes all the way back to St. Peter in the early church. The agreement was an understandable reaction to the dwindling of mainline Protestant power and influence at the end of the 20th century. Yet the attempt to cling to the outer church was a result of our misunderstanding of what the inner church was. As Melanchthon said, it's just the gospel and the resulting faith, and it stands forever. It's strong enough to bear the weight of seismic changes in our culture.

Back in the 1990s, something was afoot that few people recognized. These kinds of ecumenical agreements were built on functioning denominations that people thought still mattered like they did back in the '50s. Those were the heady days when accounts of church history across denominations in this country were all about mergers, growth, and ecumenical agreements. But already in the 1990s, the day of denominations was over. The outer church never lasts. It never holds sway. But as the Danish theologian N. F. S. Grundtvig's hymn asserts, the inner church shall stand "even when steeples are falling."

It's easy to be pessimistic when you're confronted with the sheer numbers and scale of decline in denominations. When asked about their church connections, an ever-growing proportion of college students these days checks the box marked "none." Looking for life there can only draw sighs of frustration from me. Yet there is hope. There are places of faith and ferment where the inner church is a living and vital thing. There are Episcopalians who've discovered Luther and publish books and blogs, and they host a couple huge conferences each year with superb preaching and teaching. Among Lutherans, groups like 1517 are doing the same thing. Christians are finding ways to cross denominational lines to flock together as birds of a theological feather. Look there and you will see the church beginning to reassemble in ways that are similar to the early church. That's where the Holy Spirit blows about, creating faith wherever it pleases God.[3] It's just that what is pleasing to the Spirit may lie beyond structures and institutions.

The church in this country won't be bound by denominational constructs. It will organize itself around affiliations within the inner church. Where the church grows and lives will be the place where real sinners encounter radical and authentic preaching that's fearless in naming sin and declaring what Christ has done about it. But it'll be hard to map it statistically. When the church exists in the synapses, it means the church is becoming nimble enough to move like the waters are constantly shifting, as when the Spirit of God moved over the face of the deep in the beginning.

In a sermon in Leipzig when the old Roman Catholic prince died and the city became a new Lutheran stronghold, Luther talked about the church as the *Heufflein Christi*, the little band of Christians. There, grace-hardened sinners will learn to recognize one another, even as they cling to the gospel's promises. I like that image of us members of the body of Christ as being just a bunch of broken folks barely clinging to the Crucified One, who has a much stronger hold on us. Baptized, strengthened in the Lord's Supper and sustained in the proclamation of the gospel, you're in the thick of a batch of Christians who've been pulled into the inner church for Christ's sake.

---

[3] Ibid., 40 (Article V).

Chapter 8

The Word Made Visible

Once we know what the church is, we can bring the scope of our focus to a narrow topic by looking at the two sacraments by which the church delivers Christ's promise to sinners. There are actually seven articles in the Augsburg Confession that deal with the sacraments:

Article IX on baptism
Article X on the Lord's Supper
Article XI on confession
Article XII on repentance
Article XIII on the use of the sacraments
Article XXII on both kinds
Article XIV on the Mass

In order to understand what Philip Melanchthon is up to in these articles, we need a quick primer on the Scholastic theology that Luther and his fellow Reformers had been taught and that their opponents in Rome still held. The church in Rome taught that in his crucifixion and death, Christ earned everlasting merit from God, who bestowed that merit on the church. The church's job was to function as the storehouse of that merit, with the pope as vicar, seeing to it that it was all distributed properly. What was distributed was a substance, an actual thing given to repentant sinners that would counteract the effect of sin. This substance is called grace, but you might understand how it functions by calling it "oomph." You get some oomph initially in baptism to deal with original sin, and then more oomph is given to create a desire in you for both good deeds and more oomph. If you die with too little oomph, you'll die in a state of sin and go to hell. But if you've accumulated enough oomph to balance out your sins, then you'll go to heaven, or at least to purgatory, where you can work off your sins for a few thousand years.

Where the Roman church thought of this oomph, or grace, as a substance to accumulate, Luther turned this approach on its head. He regarded grace less as a thing and more as something active on God's part—it's more verb-like than noun-like. The sacraments aren't some convenience store where you can fuel your spiritual SUV or moral minivan. Instead, the sacraments are God acting in a gracious way toward you, delivering the benefits that Christ wants to give you. The word Luther used to describe the sacraments is as *testaments*, just like the Old and New Testaments. When you hear *testament*, though, you should think of "last will and testament," because the sacraments are a bestowal of an inheritance on behalf of someone who died—in this case, Jesus himself. So the essence of the sacraments is that they consist of a trustworthy promise.

In 1520, Luther wrote a treatise called "The Babylonian Captivity of the Church." In it, he established the criteria for a sacrament: First, a sacrament is commanded by Christ. Second, it bears the promise of Christ. And finally, it uses an earthly element. He went through the list of the Roman church's seven sacraments and held them up against his criteria. While they're useful, confirmation, marriage, ordination, and last rites don't qualify. Even things as great as confession and absolution are eliminated because they don't have an earthly element. The list got whittled from seven to two. And Luther argued there are two parts to our two sacraments: the Word of God and our faith in that promise. The sacraments exist at the mash-up point of these two things.

Luther insisted that the promise be declared first and then that sinners "make use" of the sacraments by faith. You make use of the sacraments by trusting God at his Word. You can even test God by examining whether God's Word actually holds true in the midst of life's worst circumstances. What's more, you're allowed to go further and demand that God be true to that promise. In other words, when life sucks you can hold God's feet to the fire—a most faithful thing—and say, "Where's that abundant life you said was coming?"

The command and promise of the sacrament of baptism are given by Christ in Matthew: "Go therefore and make disciples of all nations, baptizing them in the name of the Father and of the Son and of the Holy Spirit, and teaching them to obey everything that I have commanded you. And remember, I am with you always, to the end of the age" (28:19–20). And the earthly element, of course, is water.

There's no need for holy water. Any water will do. Clean water works to sustain the image of cleansing, but water from a mud puddle or polluted stream will work just as well. Whatever kind of water is used, because it's water, there are a number of facets to it. First it reminds us of a thirst being quenched, like Jesus promised the woman at the well in John: "Everyone who drinks this water will be thirsty again, but whoever drinks the water I give them will never thirst. Indeed, the water I give them will become in them a spring of water welling up to eternal life" (4:13 NIV). Water as your earthly element should also make you think of washing and cleansing, like the story of Naaman the leper being healed by washing in the Jordan or the victorious saints in Revelation 7:9, the host arrayed in white whose robes have been washed in the blood of the lamb. The best thing to think about when the water is poured into the font, though, is drowning and rescue. A traditional baptismal font has eight sides, one each for Noah and the seven others who were in the ark in the Flood (though the symbol doesn't really work if baptism is about *death* and resurrection and Noah and his family didn't have to die).

Because baptism is about the promise and our trust in it, it's about an event when the relationship between God and a sinner began, as well as an *ongoing* baptismal life that continues long beyond the sprinkling, pouring, or immersion in water. Baptism can be thought of in the past tense, in the sense of the water having been poured. But baptism is most importantly something happening in present tense, because the promise and our return to it continue. The baptismal life was begun, but it *does* go on. We rightly declare, "I *am* baptized." This counters the view of baptism held by Luther's opponents in the Roman church, who saw the sacrament as an entrance rite where you then have access to all that oomphy grace. A baptized life in that approach, then, meant two things: first, taking part in the church's other six sacraments (especially the sacrifice of the Mass and penance) and, second, proving your faith and accumulating more grace through acts of charity.

Baptism as an ongoing relationship, begun with the water and the word, also counters the position of the Anabaptists on the other side of the church from Luther's Roman opponents. They argued for a believer's baptism. For them, baptism was a seal on faith already present, which they said a baby can't possibly have. And the life of faith meant making a personal decision for baptism, acting to turn your life over to God, and then striving to live a pure and moral life. This turned the actor in baptism from God to you. And that meant what your baptism is can shift and change. It took the dependability of baptism away.

But Luther's view of baptism always saw it relationally. In the water and the word of promise, God established that relationship. As Romans says,

> Don't you know that all of us who were baptized into Christ Jesus were baptized into his death? We were therefore buried with him through baptism into death in order that, just as Christ was raised from the dead through the glory of the Father, we too may live a new life. For if we have been united with him in a death like his, we will certainly also be united with him in a resurrection like his.
>
> For we know that our old self was crucified with him so that the body ruled by sin might be done away with, that we should no longer be slaves to sin. (6:3–5 NIV)

It's all about the very worst thing we imagine for ourselves: our ignominy and the utter defeat of death are linked to the best thing about Christ—his suffering and death for you. The way you get saved in baptism is to be drowned, to die to yourself, and then be given the life of the resurrection.

As Paul also says in Galatians, "For freedom Christ has set us free. Stand firm, therefore, and do not submit again to a yoke of slavery" (5:1). This relationship of death and resurrection in baptism is a relationship of freedom and for- giveness that bestows a future. It declares that no longer will your identity and future be dependent on your past, your actions, your failures and foibles, your good intentions, or your deciding anything about Jesus. Instead, this baptismal life is eschatological. It comes crashing in from the future. In baptism, the judgment that God will make on you on the Last Day is declared well in advance. The baptismal life is how the predestination Paul points to in Romans 8 works. God's promise will *not* be thwarted.

If this is what God's doing in baptism, then confessing your sins and hearing the absolution is merely a continuation of the present tense life of baptism. And so is the Lord's Supper. Among many congregations today, there's been some debate about whether it's kosher to issue an open invitation to everyone present, baptized or not, to take part in Communion. But if the delivery of the promise of forgiveness of sins in the sacrament is an extension of the baptismal life, then the Lord's Supper is a sacrament intended to nourish that baptismal relationship. The Lord's Supper is for the baptized.

This isn't exclusionary. In fact, it's exactly how things worked in the early church. Everyone was welcome to take part in the worship service, but when they got to Communion, those who weren't baptized left. This was an evangelistic practice that we're hard put to understand in a society bent on individual freedom and instant gratification. But the purpose here was to say, "We want you to be a part of this, so let's talk about baptism. And then when you've been linked to Christ's death and resurrection, those promises will be nurtured in this way."

Really, the best way to live your baptismal life is to take a look at yourself and say, "Ah, crap! I did it again. I'm powerless over myself. I'm thankful you're at the wheel, Jesus, because I'm a horrible driver of my life." Or as Luther said in the Small Catechism, baptism means that "the old creature in us with all sins and evil desires is to be drowned and die through daily contrition and repentance, and on the other hand that daily a new person is to come forth and rise up to live before God in righteousness and purity forever."[1] In the very first thesis of the Ninety-Five Theses, Luther said, "When our Lord and Master Jesus Christ said, 'Repent,' he

[1] Luther, "Small Catechism," 360.

willed the entire life of believers to be one of repentance."[2] Baptism is *ongoing*. It's not a once-and-done kind of thing. It's constantly returning to your Lord for forgiveness and freedom.

When Luther began writing "The Babylonian Captivity of the Church," he initially said there were three sacraments: penance (confession and absolution), baptism, and the Lord's Supper. But by the end of his treatise, he'd eliminated penance from the list. He saw it as merely an extension of the ongoing relationship established in baptism. Christians need to keep clinging to the very promise declared in the water and the word: you are mine and you are forgiven for Christ's sake.

That's why it's so hard for pastors when members approach them to ask if they could get the grandkids baptized when they come home for Thanksgiving. Their kids seem to have turned their back on the church these members raised them in and treat the faith as meaningless. They come to the pastor out of great love and concern for the grandchildren, wanting to make sure the little ones don't go to hell because they haven't been baptized. Surely baptizing those kids is not to be denied. Why would anyone ever want to prevent this gift from being given? But a pastor also has to think about the post-dunking life of faith. How will the promises delivered in the baptism be continually given so that faith in them grows?

Baptism isn't magic, and we ought not treat it superstitiously. It's not the absence of the sacrament that condemns us; it's our contempt for the promise attached to it that keeps us from having what the sacrament wants to give. When grandparents have come to me, I've always said, "Yes, we'll baptize those wonderful kids." And then I follow it by

---

[2] Martin Luther, "Ninety-Five Theses," in *Luther's Works*, 31:25.

saying, "And when we do, you need to know you're commit-
ting to making sure in every way possible that those grand-
babies keep hearing about their baptism and about what
Jesus has done for them."

Isn't that why we light a candle and give it to the one
baptized, even adults? We encourage them to live for others:
"Let your light so shine before others that they may see your
good works and glorify your Father in heaven." But really
what we're doing with the candle is giving them an annual
reminder of the promise: "Jesus is the light of the world.
He claimed you in your baptism." And if you want to be
reminded even more frequently of what God has declared
about you, then when you're standing naked in the shower,
make the sign of the cross and say out loud, "I *am* baptized."
Because you are. The next time you pass a baptismal font,
dip a finger in the font, make a cross on your forehead,
and say those words: "I am baptized." You can count on it
because the one who made the promise, Jesus Christ crucified, is the same yesterday, today, and forever. Nothing can
separate you from the love of God in Christ Jesus.

Chapter 9

Sacraments Valid and Effective

For Melanchthon, Luther, and their fellow Reformers in the ever-widening Wittenberg circle, the main thing in the sacraments was God's promise in Christ Jesus. The promise is attached to an earthly element and given to us sinners in the sacraments. In baptism, the promise of life, salvation, and deliverance from the devil, the world, and our sinful selves comes with Jesus' words in Matthew: "Remember, I am with you always, to the end of the age" (28:20). When faith grabs hold of the promise given with the water in baptism, not only is the sacrament valid; it's also effective. That means that speaking the formula, "In the name of the Father, and of the Son, and of the Holy Spirit," as part of a baptism makes for a sacrament rightly performed. But it's the trust in the promise that makes for a sacrament that *does* what it's given to do.

When faith happens, then the Holy Spirit begins the work prayed for in our standard offertory: "Create in me a clean heart, O God, and renew a right spirit within me. Cast me not away from your presence, and take not your Holy Spirit from me. Restore unto me the joy of thy salvation.

And uphold me with thy free spirit." In that, we can say that baptism is truly a death and resurrection, for it goes after the old sinful person in us, who doesn't believe or trust in anyone but ourselves to achieve our self-continuity project. We are for all intents and purposes drowned and raised from the dead with our lungs now full of the breath of the Holy Spirit—divine mouth-to-mouth between God and the lifeless one. We find that in the sacraments, God comes to us to bring about the divine declaration spoken at the end of the sixth day: that he saw that it was very good.

Although our first parents in the Garden of Eden thought they could claim the knowledge of good and evil by eating the fruit of the forbidden tree, the whole rest of the book of Genesis reveals that God has allowed no such thing. At the end of Genesis, poor put-upon Joseph finally meets up with his dastardly brothers. They had done him dirty time and again, including staging his death in an attack by wild dogs and selling him into slavery in Egypt because they hated him so much. Along the way, he was able to interpret dreams and wound up using that gift not only to deliver people from the ravages of famine but also to rise in power to the point of becoming Pharaoh's right-hand slave. When his brothers' families suffered from the famine back home in Canaan, they came to Egypt with empty baskets, begging for grain to take home to their families.

Joseph connived to get them accused of theft, and in the big reveal, these epitomes of sibling rivalry begged for their little brother's forgiveness. Joseph had been blessed with the ability to know there is more than what meets the eye when he interpreted dreams. But he responded to their gutless begging by saying, "Who am I to determine what should be forgiven? I don't know the difference between right and wrong. When you did such malicious things to me and our poor grieving father, you did it for evil. But God used it for good, to save me and to save so many in this famine." In First

Corinthians, Paul echoes Joseph when he says that "now we see in a mirror, dimly, but then we will see face to face" (13:12). He claims that we, too, don't know good from evil. We can't judge what's what.

The story of the Bible is one in which God's human creatures are continually beset by the temptation to claim knowledge and power. The Israelites in the Old Testament and the disciples, apostles, and first believers in the New Testament all have the same vision problem as the blind man in Mark whom Jesus only partly heals. He says, "I see people, but they look like trees walking around." The temptation for us is to listen to the loudest voices that bid us to look out for number one, pull ourselves up by our own bootstraps, and be all we can be. How many times have we heard the bromide that if you just work hard enough, you can achieve anything? Or that you can be anything you want to be? That works pretty well until you face woes like Job's or those that are found in so many of our families: awful divorces, life as a single parent, some economic earthquake like job loss, disability from a work injury, or constant and chronic pain. When someone has more than three strikes against them, try telling them they can be anything they want to be.

If baptism declares Christ's promise to be with us, to deliver us, to give us life and give it abundantly, then how is anyone facing the reality of brokenness and death that lies under the surface in our lives ever able to sustain a trust in that promise? This is where the Sacrament of the Altar comes in. It's the sacrament that works to nurture and sustain the faith in the promise, the faith that so often hangs by the slimmest of threads. The articles dealing with this sacrament in the Augsburg Confession are Article X on the Lord's Supper, Article XIII on the use of the sacrament, Article XXII on both kinds, and Article XXIV on the Mass. In all these articles, Melanchthon shows how Luther and the other Reformers sought to protect the delivery of the promise so that sinners can effectively have what Christ set out to give.

The Lord's Supper, of course, has its roots in the annual Jewish festival of Passover. After Joseph's family came to Egypt for grain, they all wound up living there and eventually were enslaved. God sought the Israelites' freedom by sending Moses to demand freedom from Pharaoh through the give-and-take of the 10 plagues. The final plague was the death of the firstborn across Egypt. God told Moses the Israelites could be spared from the Angel of Death by slaughtering a lamb and daubing the posts and lintels of their doors with its blood. Then death would pass over that house. Every year since then, Jews have remembered the Passover by gathering for a family meal, not unlike the Thanksgiving spread you no doubt dine on. This seder feast featured the same menu as was eaten so long before in the days when their ancestors cried salty tears and tasted the bitterness of slavery.

The last week of his life, on the night when Judas betrayed him, Jesus gathered with his disciples for the same meal. At the end of the meal, Jesus took the leftovers on the table and changed the entire festival. The Passover is a remembrance of the past. It looked backward to a thing God had done. But now Jesus turned the meal into something eschatological. It became a piece of the Supper of the Lamb at the end of days, when his victory over death comes in its fullness. The eating and drinking of the bread and wine became a new kind of remembering.

Think of it as re-*member*ing: putting the pieces together in a new and unexpected way. We do this for the remembrance of him, in order to remember in the ancient way of remembering, doing it as an ongoing and also new thing, because of Christ's promise that creates a future unbound by the past. There's an echo here of what we've already seen in baptism. We said we can talk about our baptism in the past tense—"I was baptized"—because of the event of the physical element that was used in the past. But much more, we can talk about our baptism using present tense—"I *am* baptized"—because the promise endures beyond the initial pouring. The promise of Jesus' choosing you, of God's electing activity in the sacrament, goes on beyond whatever date is on your baptismal certificate. In the upper room in Jerusalem, Jesus refused to make your future and your identity hinge on the past. Instead, he makes it present and real for you today.

The moves Melanchthon made in the sacramental articles in the Augsburg Confession came in order to preserve both parts of the Lord's Supper. Article X says, "[Our churches] teach that the body and blood of Christ are truly present and are distributed to those who eat in the Supper of the Lord."[1] In Article XXII, he argues for distributing *both* the bread and wine in Communion, because that was what Jesus commanded at the Last Supper. Those two articles show what happens in the sacrament and what the bread and wine are. In Article XIII and Article XXIV, we see a push back against the corruption of the sacrament in the Roman church's practices. These articles work to preserve the promise attached to the earthly elements.

Over the centuries, the church had stopped giving people the cup of wine in communion. Only the priest was allowed to drink it. That set up a hierarchy in the sacrament, and the Reformers in Wittenberg had already begun offering both the bread and wine again a decade earlier while Luther was in hiding in the Wartburg castle. The argument Luther made in "The Babylonian Captivity of the Church" was that if Jesus commanded us to give the bread and wine

---

[1] Melanchthon, "Augsburg Confession," 45.

to be eaten and drunk, we'd darn well better give both bread *and* wine, whether people want to partake of either.

In the Small Catechism, Luther argued that the eating and drinking aren't the main things in the sacrament of the altar. Instead, the main thing is the words "given and shed for you." The eating and the drinking happen in order to give you the forgiveness of sins—that is, to give you the one thing that can provide you the clarity of vision needed to believe and trust your Lord. Article XIII says the sacraments aren't "instituted . . . only to be marks of profession among men."[2] They're not given as metrics for us to be able to decide who's in and who's out. Instead, the sacraments are "signs and testimonies of the will of God toward us, intended to arouse and strengthen faith in those who use them. Accordingly, sacraments are to be used so that faith, which believes the promises offered and displayed through the sacraments, may increase."[3]

Even some Lutheran hymnals get confused on this count. Liturgical purists and advocates of high church worship wanted Lutherans to come in line with the historical liturgies of what we call the Western or Latin Rite. That means they insisted that our communion liturgy include a long prefatory prayer over the bread and wine. The words of institution are included as part of the Eucharistic Prayer. These words, though, *aren't* a prayer:

> In the night in which he was betrayed, our Lord Jesus Christ, took bread, broke it, and gave it to his disciples, saying, "Take and eat. This is my body given for you. Do this for the remembrance of me." Again, after supper, he took the cup, gave thanks and gave it to them saying, "This cup is the new

[2] Ibid., 47.

[3] Ibid.

testament in my blood, given and shed for you for the forgiveness of sins. Do this for the remembrance of me."

These words are direct proclamation. By inserting them into a prayer directed to God, rather than to the sinners they're intended to be spoken to, we make the sacrament into a messy mishmash.

It's all part of the problem of figuring out how all this happens. Those words, "This is my body" and "This is my blood," have caused controversy for Christians for hundreds of years. Here's how it works. Think of a young Christian, a college student who would fit in my classrooms and who has grown into his full manhood. (We can only hope that he's grown anyway. If he'd been born his current size, his birth would have been an unholy event for his mother.) Somewhere along the way, Christian's voice changed, he shot up a few feet, he grew hair in the sweatier regions of his body, and he began to spend a few dollars over the years on razor blades and shaving cream. But every step of the way, even though his external qualities have changed, Christian has always been Christian.

The philosophical language for that is that Christian's substance has remained the same while his accidence has changed. The Scholastic theologians like Thomas Aquinas borrowed those terms from Aristotle and applied them to the sacrament. They said that unlike Christian, the accidence of the bread and wine stays the same while its substance changes. It still looks like bread and wine, but now its substance is Jesus' actual body and blood. The term for this is *transubstantiation. Trans* means "change." *Substance* is right there in the word. So it's the process by which the substance of the elements in the Lord's Supper is changed. The way it happens is that a man whose been ordained by a bishop in historic succession has had hands laid on him. He's ontologically changed—his own substance is changed—and now he can say the words and turn bread and wine into flesh and blood. What's more, what happens in the sacrament is that Jesus' suffering and death on Calvary were not once and for all. Instead, with Jesus' body and blood in front of us now, the priest resacrifices Jesus. The promise isn't enough, and the sacrifice, the breaking of Jesus' body, has to be done over and over again.

The primary point of Article XXIV is to defend the changes Luther and the Reformers made in the worship service. The whole aim of worship shifted away from the idea of a sacrifice that we and the priest make in order to earn merit before God and toward the proclamation of a promise in which Christ does what he declares: claim you, forgive you, deliver you, give you life, and give it abundantly. For the Reformers, the problem with this Scholastic view of the sacrament, which they kind of pussyfoot around in these articles, is that it all depends on a superstitious view of both the sacrament and the vocation of a pastor. There's no need for this supposed magic. The words of institution bear their own power. They give what they say.

They're first-order discourse—language that does something, words that give what they offer. Words like "I love you" and "I forgive you" work this same way. Inserting the words of institution in a prayer that is taken from the Roman sacramental system winds up being a betrayal of what the Reformers gave their lives up for. Explicitly or not, intended or not, it makes the proclamation into a sort of incantation. That's why, when I preside at the sacrament, I slice away the hoo-ha and get down to business. You'll get the words of institution, unadorned by prayers, petitions, and raising up the loaf and cup.

The other view of the sacrament that Melanchthon was contending with came from the Swiss Reformer Zwingli (and later Calvin)—the 16th-century forbear of the Reformed churches and lots of other Protestant denominations.

Zwingli argued that when Jesus declared the bread and wine were his body and blood, the Lord meant that they were symbols of his body and blood. Zwingli thought Jesus had ascended into heaven and couldn't be in two places at once. For him the bread and wine have to be merely a symbol we apprehend in faith. In a way, our faith takes us spiritually to where Jesus is, because the signs of the bread and wine point us there. Luther debated with Zwingli about this and grabbed a piece of chalk and wrote on the table between them, *Hoc est*, "This *is*." Luther couldn't abide not thinking Jesus would be true to his promise to be present in the bread and wine. This is why Melanchthon nonchalantly declared Jesus to be there promising us forgiveness of sins, so that faith happens. Lutherans talk about the "real presence" of Christ in the sacrament. Christ is "in, with, and under" the bread and wine, because his promise has been attached to the elements.

One practical consequence of this is the need to do some hard thinking about how we've made the sacraments about us and our perceived needs. We've created a sacramental smorgasbord of bread, gluten-free wafers, wine and grape juice, common cup, divided common cup, little trays of tiny glasses, and even mail-order Communion. But if the main thing in the sacrament is the promise, that means that if your digestive tract can't deal with gluten, we don't offer yet another option. If you can't drink the wine because you're working a 12-step program, we don't offer a nonalcoholic choice. Instead, we teach people to zero in on the main thing, the promise declared in the words of institution: given and shed *for you*. And we invite people forward to receive that promise, because it carries the same weight and power, with or without both elements. The genie is out of the bottle, and by wanting to peddle softly for the sake of people's feelings, we've diluted the power of the sacrament. We've become grand prestidigitators doing a bit of sacramental sleight-of-hand, misdirecting people from the very promise that needs to be the focus of the sacrament.

But if we're going to line up in the tradition laid out by Melanchthon (and your church constitution demands that you do), then it's time to think seriously about how we ensure both the validity and efficacy of the sacraments.

Chapter 10

It'll Be the Death of You

When I was ordained as a pastor, I was asked a number of questions about how I intended to comport myself in my vocation. I vowed to be diligent in studying the scriptures, to pray for those I'd serve, to administer the sacraments, and all the things that should go without saying or vowing for someone who hopes to serve as one of the church's public proclaimers. But there's a sneaky little line tucked into those questions that asks if I acknowledge the Lutheran Confessions as a true witness and faithful account of the gospel found in the scripture. My answer to each question, including that one, was "I will, and I ask God to help me."

The act of signing on the dotted line for the confessions is known as subscription, and the Augsburg Confession called for the same thing from the Reformers in 1530. Luther's elector, John of Saxony, along with the elector's brother John Frederick and princes like Philip of Hesse, as well as representatives of two free imperial cities all subscribed to the document, just like John Hancock and other who wrote their names at the bottom of the Declaration of

Independence in 1776. The act of signing on to the content of a document like that was a life-or-death matter for them.

Five years before Augsburg, Luther preached at the funeral of his elector Frederick the Wise, the prince who had stood by Luther at the Diet of Worms while his Wittenberg professor gave his famous "Here I Stand" speech. In his sermon, Luther said Frederick had suffered two deaths. The elector's big death came first:

> Following Christ, he died two years ago in Augsburg and suffered the real death. . . . There our beloved elector openly confessed Christ's death and resurrection before the whole world and he stuck to it, staking his land and people, indeed his own body and life, upon it.[1]

This is "the death in which we would rather risk our neck, if this were possible, before we would deny the man who is called Jesus Christ," while the other physical death "is only a childish death or an animal death."[2] When you've gone through the big death, then physical death is a small matter:

> When it happens, as it did with our beloved prince, that the body merely lies upon the bed and there is no fright and trembling, because he was called into Christ's kingdom through baptism and afterwards openly confessed Christ and listened with all diligence and his whole heart to God's Word, and thus only the five senses died away—then this is the least of death and only half of death.[3]

---

[1] Martin Luther, "Two Funeral Sermons, 1532," in *Luther's Works: Sermons I* (Philadelphia: Fortress, 1959), 51:237.

[2] Ibid., 238.

[3] Ibid.

It's as if God were saying, "So now I will send death to you only in the sense that you will die as far as your five senses are concerned, as in a sleep."

The gospel that the Augsburg Confession proclaims certainly has to do with our last breath, God's final judgment, and our ultimate destination in God's eternal reign. But like the signers and Frederick, each moment we face brings us to the big death, the question of whether this is true. Big identity questions are involved, each of which aims at the three places our relationships take shape: "Who am I?" focuses on my standing *coram deo*, in connection to God. "Who is my neighbor?" looks at my standing *coram hominibus*, in connection to those who make up my web of family, friends, colleagues, and fellow human beings. "What is God up to in the world?" causes me to check on my standing *coram mundo*, in relation to the creation God has placed me in.

Like death and resurrection themselves, the answers to these questions don't happen because of a decision or some ginning up of my vaunted free will. No, my true identity arrives on account of the Holy Spirit's work not just bringing me to faith but keeping me in the faith in the very moment when the questions are foisted upon me. In his explanation of the third article of the Apostles' Creed in the Small Catechism, Luther showed how it works:

> I believe that by my own understanding or strength I cannot believe in Jesus Christ my LORD or come to him, but instead the Holy Spirit has called me through the gospel, enlightened me with his gifts, made me holy and kept me in the true faith, just as he calls, gathers, enlightens, and makes holy the whole Christian church on earth and keeps it with Jesus Christ in the one common, true faith.[4]

---

[4] Luther, "Small Catechism," 355–56.

An honest assessment of our own will and abilities will lead us to admit that we can't possibly justify ourselves or save ourselves from sin. This is why the response to all the questions at ordination is always "I will, and I ask God to help and guide me." I want to be faithful in the three *coram*'s. I see through a glass dimly and can tell there's something there I want. But it lies beyond my reach, and I don't have it in me to get it, so if anything's going to happen, the Holy Spirit needs to make it happen in me. With each moment and encounter, God will have to make the big death of faith happen. Life is lived in this tension between faith and unfaith. Life is lived in the dynamic push-pull between my self-centered desires and my neighbor's needs. Life is lived in the breach between death and resurrection.

We can see it happen in the witness of our forebears along 2,000 years of the church's history. It's there in the vivid stories of the saints and martyrs. Paul himself, the greatest evangelist of the early church, confessed in Romans, "For I do not do the good I want, but the evil I do not want is what I do" (7:19). On the verge of turning to Christianity after long years of exploring various bodies of theological and philosophical thought (and other sorts of bodies), Augustine prayed, "God grant me chastity. But not yet." He knew how ungraspable God's desired holiness was for him. People like the martyr Paolo Miki, who was crucified for his faith in late-medieval Japan, or Charles Lwanga, who was thrown into a furnace for not renouncing his faith, would not have sought praise for their resistance, for it was Christ alone whom they saw as praiseworthy.

Starting with the Edict of Worms in 1521, it became illegal to hold to the teaching of Luther and his Wittenberg circle. Not only was Luther wanted dead or alive; anyone who associated with him faced the same condemnation. From the most visible evangelical partisans like Luther and Melanchthon to second-tier folks like Johannes Brenz, Wolfgang Capito, and Argula von Grumbach to the first evangelical martyrs who were burned at the stake in the low countries, each person became a public witness. As soon as they opened their mouths to preach or defend other Reformers or had a word published, they risked life and limb. Their old lives were as good as dead, but they saw themselves as having been raised to new life by the newly unbound gospel.

It need not be so dramatic as the danger faced by the martyrs or by threats from the 16th-century political and church realms. Our own witness is found in the death and resurrection of vocation—the various callings God places us in to serve in the world: being a parent, a neighbor, a citizen, a freeway driver, and even a social media maven. This passel of vocations is organic. It's relational. It's anything *but* something attained by my own understanding or effort.

Ultimately, the work of Melanchthon and Luther and all those signatories was to proclaim the gospel of Jesus Christ to you in such a way that the Holy Spirit grabs hold. So you will be raised from your moment-by-moment big death. So your neighbor will be taken care of as a preview of coming attractions—that is, of the new heaven and earth of the "youngest day." So your last breath will be a little death. The old will have passed away. No regrets, for looking back, you'll see God in the rearview mirror, just where he likes to be seen. It's no different from Moses seeing God from the safety of the cleft in the rock on Mount Sinai: "Objects in mirror are closer than they appear." And you can face the end as a new beginning, just like Paul in Romans: "I am convinced that neither death, nor life, nor angels, nor rulers, nor things present, nor things to come, nor powers, nor height, nor depth, nor anything else in all creation, will be able to separate us from the love of God in Christ Jesus our Lord" (8:38–39).

The Augsburg Confession was originally just one political document among many set to type in the printshops that

had sprung up across Germany during the Reformation, but
its power and legacy are so much greater. The presentation
of Melanchthon's work at the Diet of Augsburg on June 25,
1530, was a mere moment. But the Spirit's work in and
through it continues. At its core the confession assures that
those who've answered, "I will, and I ask God to help me"
will do all they can to deliver the gospel in such a way that
Jesus' death and resurrection become "for you." That's what
our Lord has been after all along. To be bound to you so
tightly that you can't spot where Jesus ends and you begin.
To bind you to your neighbor so tightly that you're com-
pelled to serve. To create a new you that's another piece of
the structure of the New Jerusalem.

How it happens involves no cookie cutters or machine
work, for the New Jerusalem is adorned with all kinds of
jewels, each having undergone a transformation through the
catalyst of daily death and resurrection. The great hymn
that used to be sung at the funerals of old Norwegians in
the Minnesota congregation where I served as a youth minister asks, "Who is this host arrayed in white?" Revelation
answers that "these are they who have come out of the great
ordeal; they have washed their robes and made them white
in the blood of the Lamb" (7:14). You are arrayed in white
because of the big death that started in your baptism and
will continue beyond this life's demands.

Those who have died and been raised have the mantle
of eternity as their baptismal gown and funeral pall. Article
by article, the Augustana declares God's "for you-ness."
In the face of such immense grace and mercy, and aware
of your own sin, you will respond. And God will help and
guide you.